£1·75

MAHATMA GANDHI

THE MAN AND HIS MESSAGE

Donn Byrne

MODERN ENGLISH
PUBLICATIONS

This edition published 1987
Reprinted 1988

ISBN 0 906149 45 2

Typesetting and Make up: *Quadra Graphics, Oxford*
Printed in Hong Kong

The photograph on page (iv) is reproduced by courtesy of Camera
Press. The photographs between pages 36 and 37 are reproduced
by courtesy of Camera Press (head of Gandhi, Gandhi spinning);
Keystone Press (Gandhi in South Africa, Gandhi and millworkers);
BBC Hulton Picture Library (the Salt March) and the Mansell
Collection (Gandhi with Nehru, Gandhi lying in state).
The quotations on page iv are taken from *Talking of Gandhi* by
Francis Watson and Hallam Tennyson, Sangam Books 1976,
incorporating material originally published by Orient Longman in
1957.

Contents

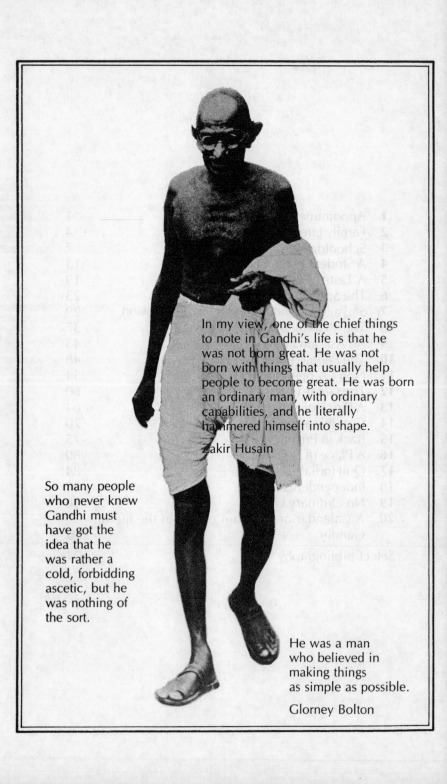

In my view, one of the chief things to note in Gandhi's life is that he was not born great. He was not born with things that usually help people to become great. He was born an ordinary man, with ordinary capabilities, and he literally hammered himself into shape.

Zakir Husain

So many people who never knew Gandhi must have got the idea that he was rather a cold, forbidding ascetic, but he was nothing of the sort.

He was a man who believed in making things as simple as possible.

Glorney Bolton

1

Appointment with Death

It was Friday, January 30th, 1948: just a few months after India had finally become independent.

Gandhi got up early as usual, at about 3.30 am. He prayed, had his bath, and then began work. He also studied Bengali, one of the many languages spoken in India, for about an hour. Gandhi had only recently returned to Delhi, where he was staying at the house of a rich friend, Ghanshyam Das Birla, and when he was free to go back to Bengal, he wanted to be able to speak to the people there in their own language.

The morning passed. Gandhi had a simple meal of fruit, cooked and raw vegetables and some goat's milk. Then he slept for an hour.

Late in the afternoon an old friend, Sardar Patel, came to see him. The two had known each other since the early days of the struggle for independence. Patel was now the Deputy Prime Minister of India, but it was rumoured that he did not get on well with Jawaharlal Nehru, the Prime Minister. Gandhi desperately wanted the two men to agree, for the good of the country. He had already written to Nehru about this problem, and now he was trying to convince Patel.

Meanwhile, as the two men talked on, Abha — one of Gandhi's two great-nieces who looked after him — hovered around anxiously. Gandhi was due to go to a prayer meeting, and he was, already late. Abha was Gandhi's 'timekeeper'. She tried to get Gandhi to look at his big pocket watch. But she could not bring herself to interrupt this important discussion, so the two men talked on.

1

At last Gandhi said goodbye to Patel and got ready to leave. The prayer meeting was only a short distance away, in the gardens of Birla House. But Gandhi was an old man now, weakened by his latest fast from which he was now trying to recover, and he could no longer walk easily without the help of Abha and his other great-niece, Manu.

"My two walking-sticks!" Gandhi used to call them affectionately.

He joked with the two girls as the three of them made their way towards the prayer meeting, but he was also a little impatient. He felt that they were not walking fast enough.

"Let's hurry," Gandhi told them. "We're late, and you know I don't like to keep people waiting."

All his life, Gandhi had tried to be punctual . . .

The huge garden was crowded with people who had come to attend the daily prayer meeting and to see Gandhi. Excitement grew as he approached.

"Mahatma Gandhi ki jai!" the crowd shouted. "Long live Mahatma Gandhi!"

Gandhi had nearly died during his latest fast, and everyone was happy to see 'Bapu' again — the 'father' of their country.

The crowd drew back to let them pass, and he was now only a few yards from the wooden platform, from which he was going to lead the prayers.

As he approached the platform, a young man stepped out of the crowd. He put the palms of his hands together in front of him in the traditional Hindu greeting.

Gandhi paused and smiled.

The young man then bent down, as if to show the mahatma even greater respect by touching his feet. Abha tried to prevent him, but the young man brushed her aside.

Then, before anyone realised what was happening, the young man took out a small pistol, which he had kept hidden between the palms of his hands, and

2

pointed it at Gandhi. He fired three shots. Each one found its mark.

Gandhi's body crumpled, and blood seeped through his spotless white clothes.

"*He Rama!*" he cried as he fell to the ground. "Oh God!"

Gandhi died almost at once.

2
Family Life

Mohandas Karamchand Gandhi was born on October 2nd, 1869, in Porbandar, a small seatown on the Arabian Sea in Western India. At that time Porbandar was the capital of a tiny princely state, where Gandhi's father was *diwan*, the ruler's prime minister and chief adviser. The Gandhis had been in government service for more than a generation, although strictly speaking they were merchants and farmers, of the Vaisya caste. In fact, the name *gandhi* means 'grocer' in Gujarati, which is the language spoken in that part of India.

Karamchand, Gandhi's father, was not highly educated. He could read and write, but knew little history and geography. But he had a reputation for being incorruptible and tactful, although he sometimes found it difficult to accept that the British were the real power behind the princely throne.

Karamchand had been married four times. Two of his wives had died, the third was childless and Gandhi himself was the youngest son of the fourth and last wife, Putlibai. Gandhi was devoted to his mother, and she was a great influence on his life.

Putlibai was a kind, simple woman, who never learned to read and write. The two most important things in her life were her family and her religion. She took over and looked after her husband's already numerous family, cooking and working for all of them and nursing them when they fell ill. Nursing was something she especially enjoyed. 'Moniya' (as Gandhi was often called as a child) followed her example, and at one time even considered becoming a doctor.

4

Putlibai was an extremely devout woman. She prayed before every meal and, in spite of all the work she had to do in the house, found time to visit the temple every day. She fasted a good deal too, especially at Chaturmas, which is a period like Lent during the rainy season of the monsoon. During Chaturmas, Putlibai allowed herself only one meal a day.

One year, as Gandhi relates in his autobiography, *The Story of My Experiments with Truth*, Putlibai announced to her family that she would only eat on days when the sun shone. It was probably her way of trying to help the farmers: they needed rain, but they also needed sun at the time of the monsoon, so Putlibai wanted to support them through fasting and prayer.

But, she also told her family, she had to see the sun for herself before she would take any food.

Her children were very worried when they heard this. Putlibai was not strong and they were afraid that she might die if she did not eat. Besides, she spent all her time working indoors. How could she hope to see the sun if she never came out of the house?

In the end, the children decided to wait outside and keep looking for the sun themselves. Then, as soon as the watery sun appeared between the clouds, they used to dash into the house and call their mother out to see it.

But Putlibai was in no hurry. She used to finish whatever she was doing before she followed her children outside — and by that time the sun had sometimes already disappeared behind the clouds again.

"It doesn't matter," Putlibai would say. "God didn't want me to eat today."

Putlibai was a strict orthodox Hindu and never questioned what her religion taught her. According to Hinduism, for example, many people in India were 'untouchable'. These people did not belong to one of

5

the four castes: the *Brahmans*, who were priests and scholars; the *Kshatriyas*, who were soldiers and rulers; the *Vaisyas* (Gandhi's own caste), who were farmers and traders, and the *Sudras*, who were labourers.

The 'untouchables' had no caste. They were the lowest of the low; they swept the streets and did all the dirty jobs in the house. They were untouchable because they were regarded as unclean. They could therefore contaminate a person or food through contact. And, if this happened, the contamination had to be cleansed through a ritual of prayer and bathing.

Putlibai believed in these ideas just like other orthodox Hindus of the time. For her, such beliefs were part of her religion.

Gandhi's lifelong struggle against the idea of 'untouchability' began with an act of youthful rebellion. He used to play with the 'sweeper boy', who was called Uka. Uka was, of course, an 'untouchable'.

One day, Putlibai caught the two boys playing together, and she was very angry with her son.

"What are you doing?" she shouted at him. "Go and have a bath and say some prayers! And don't ever let me catch you playing with Uka again!"

Gandhi was puzzled.

"But why can't I play with Uka?" he asked. "He's just like a brother. And I don't see why I should have a bath. Uka isn't dirty!"

Just like a brother! Putlibai was horrified. She tried to explain things to her son.

"I'm not saying that Uka is a bad boy," she said. "But he's untouchable . . . and he's different from us."

Gandhi listened, but secretly he remained unconvinced. And, whenever his mother was not looking, he went on playing with Uka.

Quite early on in his life, he began his long campaign to break down the barriers of caste and to get rid of untouchability. He even found a new name for the untouchables. He called them 'Harijans'.

'Harijans' means 'Children of God.'

6

3
Schooldays in India

When Gandhi was seven, his family moved to the neighbouring state of Rajkot, where his father had become *diwan*. Here Gandhi first began to attend primary school. 'I was a mediocre student,' he wrote about himself in later years. 'My intellect must have been sluggish and my memory raw.'

Yet, in spite of this harsh assessment of himself, it would seem that he was not a bad student. At least he won several prizes. But he was always shy and sensitive, running home as soon as school was over in case 'anyone should poke fun at me'.

And he was no good at games or gymnastics. He preferred to get his exercise by going for long walks — a habit he kept up all his life. Sometimes he even went without breakfast in order to have enough time to walk to school and still be punctual — another lifelong obsession.

At the age of twelve he started at the Alfred High School, where, for the first time, he had to do all his lessons in English. This proved especially hard for Gandhi, who came from a family where no English was spoken at home.

His poor English soon got him into trouble. An English inspector came on a visit to the school and the boys were given a spelling test of five words. Gandhi spelt one of the words wrong. The teacher noticed this as he walked round the class and signalled to Gandhi to copy the word correctly from the pupil next to him. Gandhi took no notice, and was reprimanded for it later. But he did not regret what he had done.

'I never could learn the art of 'copying'!' he later said about himself.

Gandhi was only thirteen when his parents told him that he was going to be married. His bride, Kasturbai, the daughter of a Porbandar merchant, was the same age. Karsandas, one of Gandhi's brothers, was to be married at the same time. Karamchand was now nearly sixty and wanted to see his sons settled.

It was the custom in India at that time to marry young. These marriages were arranged by the parents, often when the children were little more than babies. Gandhi himself discovered that he had in fact been 'engaged' twice before, but both the girls had died.

Later in life, looking back on how he had behaved as a 'schoolboy husband', Gandhi spoke out strongly against the 'cruel custom of child marriage'. But at the time he was pleased and excited by the prospect of having a wife. It was fun, rather like getting a new playmate. Besides, he reckoned that he was lucky because Kasturbai was also a pretty girl.

After the wedding ceremony, Kasturbai came to live in the Gandhi house in Rajkot and became a member of the joint family. This meant that the young couple had a room of their own, but ate with the rest of the family. Kasturbai helped in the house, while Gandhi resumed his studies at school.

Although shy at first — his only instruction in married life was given him by his eldest brother's wife — Gandhi lost no time in assuming the role of dominant husband, as he himself admitted. From the start he tried to control Kasturbai's movements. He used to daydream about her while he was at school, and questioned her closely as soon as he came home, although she had given him no reason for jealousy. And he expected Kasturbai to give a full account of her movements.

For her part, Kasturbai resented being interrogated in

8

this way. She had no intention of telling her husband where she had been and what she had done during the day, nor did she expect to have to ask his permission before she went out — even to the temple. She deliberately took to disobeying him, refusing to answer his questions and leaving the house whenever she pleased.

Gandhi began to lose his temper with his young wife. They quarrelled, and often did not speak for days. 'Refusal to speak became the order of the day,' he commented.

Gandhi was also concerned because Kasturbai could not read or write. He tried to share with her the things he had learnt at school and often kept her awake until late into the night with his 'idle talk'. He tried to act as her teacher, but Kasturbai made little progress. She saw no reason why she should learn to read or write.

"Other Indian girls don't learn such things," she objected. "So why should I?"

When she was older, Kasturbai tried hard, again with her husband's help, to educate herself, but she never made much progress. She managed to become literate in Gujarati, her mother tongue, but never learnt more than a few words of English.

Throughout her life, however, she continued to assert her independence. She may have been a simple girl, but she had a strong will and a mind of her own.

As a boy, Gandhi had his share of petty vices. He began to smoke when he was twelve, sometimes stealing money from the house to pay for cigarettes. He also started to eat meat — in secret of course, because all his family were strict vegetarians and eating meat was regarded as a sin.

The person who persuaded him to do this was a Muslim friend, Sheik Mehtab, whose religion allowed him to eat meat. Sheik was tall, strong and very athletic, and he used to attribute all this to eating meat.

"Besides," he argued, "look at the British! They are

9

tall and strong — and they eat meat!"

There was a little poem about the British that circulated among the boys at that time. It went like this:

> Behold the mighty Englishman
> He rules the Indian small.
> Because, being a meat-eater,
> He is five cubits tall.

At that time the British ruled nearly the whole of India and also controlled the princely states, like Porbandar and Rajkot, through their political advisers. Gandhi and his fellow students would have liked to drive the British out of India, but for that they needed to be tall and strong — like the British.

At first, Gandhi was not convinced that he should eat meat. But he also worried a great deal because he was a coward — afraid of ghosts and thieves and snakes. He could not sleep without a light in his room. Even Kasturbai was braver than he was and Gandhi felt ashamed. So in the end he allowed himself to be persuaded by Sheik Mehtab, who had already convinced Gandhi's brother Karsandas to become a meat-eater.

The initiation ceremony was arranged in a lonely spot on the banks of a river just outside the town. Sheik brought along some bread and some goat's meat, and Gandhi forced himself to eat. The meat was tough, and needed a lot of chewing, but in the end Gandhi managed to swallow some.

He was immediately sick. And that night he dreamt that there was a live goat bleating away in his stomach. However, he was determined to be big and strong and brave like his friend, so he tried again. This time he had more success. After that, he continued to eat meat for a whole year, although from then on the meals were arranged in a restaurant, where Sheik and his friends sat at the table — just like Englishmen.

But in the end Gandhi had to stop eating meat, even

though he had actually begun to enjoy it. The problem was that, having eaten outside, he had no appetite for the food his mother cooked him.

"What's wrong with you?" Putlibai kept asking. "Are you ill or something?"

Gandhi could hardly admit that he had become an unholy meat-eater — in a household where not even insects were killed — so he was forced to lie. He pleaded that there was something wrong with his digestion.

But then one day the awful truth dawned on him.

"I began by eating meat," he realised. "Now I have begun to tell lies to my mother! Where will it all end?"

So he decided to give up meat-eating rather than go on deceiving his parents. He felt that he could take it up again later when his parents were dead and he would be able to do it openly. For he was still convinced that meat-eating was a good thing.

But then there was an even greater crisis in his life. His brother Karsandas had a bracelet, from which the two boys cut a piece of gold to pay off a debt. Their parents noticed that the gold was missing, but the two boys denied any knowledge of it. But this became too much for Gandhi's conscience. He felt that he had now done something really bad and that he must confess it to his father.

But how? His father was very ill at the time (his bad health had started with an accident just before Gandhi's wedding) and could hardly move from his bed. Gandhi decided to write out his confession in the form of a letter and put it in his father's hands.

Tears came into his father's eyes as he read the letter. But instead of getting angry with his son, he tore the letter up without saying a word, and Gandhi knew that he had been forgiven.

Not long after that, Karamchand died — in circumstances which his son was never able to forget.

When he came home from school, Gandhi used to

11

spend the evenings with his father, nursing him or massaging his legs until he fell asleep. He enjoyed doing this and it was also his religious duty.

But all the while he would be thinking of the moment when he would be able to get away to his room to make love to Kasturbai, who at that time was pregnant with their first child.

One evening, an uncle happened to come to the house.

"Go and rest," he told his nephew. "I'll look after your father."

Gandhi made off, eager to be with Kasturbai.

But almost immediately a servant came to the room and knocked on the door.

"Hurry!" the servant called. "Your father has been taken ill."

Puzzled, Gandhi hurried after the servant. Ill? But his father was *already* ill.

Then, as he followed the servant, the terrible truth dawned on him. His father was dead, not ill — and he had not been with him when he died. Instead, he had been making love to his pregnant wife, which was forbidden by the Hindu religion. The child — Gandhi's first son — died a few days after birth and Gandhi blamed himself for this.

'A double shame', Gandhi called this event, and he remembered it all his life.

4

A Student in London

Gandhi's family perhaps hoped that he would one day enter government service, like his father and his grandfather. He might even become *diwan*. But he needed qualifications and a family friend suggested that he should go to England to study law.

The idea must have seemed fanciful at the time, because Gandhi had finished school with mediocre marks and had just failed his first year examinations at a local college. But it caught the young Gandhi's imagination, and soon he could think of nothing else.

But there were obstacles. Money was one of them. Gandhi's father had not left the family well off when he died. But even more serious than that was his mother's opposition. In spite of the fact that the suggestion had come from a close family friend and had the support of her religious adviser. Putlibai was firmly against the idea of her son going to England. She had heard too many stories about the bad habits young men got into there: eating meat, drinking alcohol . . . and going with women.

Besides, she also felt that Gandhi's uncle should be consulted, since he was now head of the family. This uncle lived in Porbandar, so Gandhi set off to see him, even hiring a camel to get there as fast as possible. But his uncle was against the idea too . . . and was only prepared to give his consent if Putlibai agreed too!

So Gandhi hurried from one to the other, and eventually persuaded his mother to agree by taking a vow not to eat meat, not to drink alcohol and not to go with women while he was in England. And finally his

13

brother Laxmidas, who was already established as a lawyer, agreed to support Gandhi while he was in England. Gandhi had even been prepared to pawn his wife's jewels to raise the money!

But there were last minute hitches even after he had got to Bombay, where the boat to England sailed from, and had bought his ticket. He had to wait several weeks until the stormy monsoon season was over.

Meanwhile, members of his caste heard of his plans and tried to prevent him from going. No member of the Gandhi family had ever crossed the sea, they argued. It was against their religion. If he persisted in going, they would cast him out of the family.

But Gandhi's mind was made up. He had set his heart on going to England, and he was not going to let the elders stand in his way. So he was formally made an outcaste. Eventually he sailed for England on September 4 1888 — a few months after his son had been born and a few weeks before his nineteenth birthday.

Three weeks later, this timid but stubborn young man from a small provincial town in India landed at Southampton, having spent most of the voyage in his cabin, living on the food he had brought with him because he could not be sure which of the food in the ship's restaurant was vegetarian. People on board were already telling him that he should start eating meat, in order to stay alive in England, but he took no notice.

When he reached England at the end of September, the weather was already cold and wet. The other passengers were well prepared for this with warm winter clothes. Gandhi had chosen to put on his new white suit for the occasion, which he believed was the standard dress in England. It was the first of his many mistakes.

He spent the first few days in London in a large hotel near Charing Cross. But he soon realised that this was an absurd extravagance, and from there he retreated to a small squalid room in the East End of London, the poorest part of the city. There he was cold and miserable, and he desperately wanted to go back to India. But he knew that to do this would be to admit total failure.

Slowly things began to improve. He acquired a kind of guide — someone who, he said, 'initiated me into English ways and manners, and accustomed me to talking the language.' He also tried to convince him to eat meat — but Gandhi remembered the promise he had made his mother, and obstinately refused to listen to his new friend's arguments.

For a time. he lodged with an English family — a widow and her two daughters. The woman did her best to look after this strange young Indian. She cooked him plenty of vegetables but, according to him, 'the food had no taste.' The fact is he had a big appetite and he missed his spicy Indian meals. The two girls used to slip him extra slices of bread, but he was always hungry. Luckily, he found a good vegetarian restaurant where he could get the sort of meal he needed. When this happened, Gandhi felt that God himself had come to his rescue!

Gandhi found London, with its big buildings, wide streets and bustling traffic, an exciting place to be in. His term had not yet started, and he spent endless hours walking around the city.

He also liked the English and his new English friends. He was not prepared to eat meat like them, but perhaps he could do other things to make himself 'a little more English'. He worked hard to improve his knowledge of English and spent a good deal of time reading the papers. He also decided to dress in an English way.

He began to spend a lot of money on clothes. He bought a big top hat and had an expensive suit made in Bond Street. He also wore a brightly coloured tie. He walked around carrying leather gloves and a cane. In fact, in a short time he had become quite a dandy!

But, in his eagerness to ape the British, his extra-

15

vagance did not stop there. He began to study French and elocution. He bought a violin and took lessons in music. He even tried to learn how to dance, but he had no sense of rhythm and soon gave up his lessons.

Then one day he came to his senses. He realised that he was spending a lot of money — his brother's money — and he felt ashamed. Besides, he told himself, there was no reason to do all this. He was Indian, not English. When he had finished studying in England, he would go back to India, where he would spend the rest of his life. He simply did not need to imitate the British!

Gandhi sold his violin, gave up his lessons in French and elocution and changed his way of life completely. He went to live in a small room on his own. He took to walking everywhere, both to give himself exercise and to save money. He began to cook his own meals too. For breakfast he usually had porridge and cocoa, and in the evening cocoa again with bread. Only at midday did he allow himself a more substantial meal in a vegetarian restaurant.

Apart from the year when he had eaten meat as a schoolboy, Gandhi had always been a vegetarian as a matter of habit. Now he began to take a serious interest in diet and he soon became a vegetarian by conviction. Most of the new friends he made in England were enthusiastic vegetarians, and he regularly attended meetings of their societies.

He also read books about vegetarianism and began to experiment a good deal with his diet. For a time he even ate eggs because he was persuaded that they were not meat. Mostly, however, he lived on bread, fruit and vegetables. He became an expert, he records, at making carrot soup.

He also began to cut down on salt and spices — the spices he had missed so much when he first arrived from India. He had already reached the conclusion that 'the real seat of taste was not the tongue but the mind.'

By the time he had finished economising, he had

16

reduced his expenses to about fifteen shillings a week — about the same level as many other poor Indian students in London. He kept a strict record of everything he spent, doing his accounts for the day just before he went to bed. It was a practice he kept up so long as he continued to earn money, and he strongly recommended it to everyone.

While he was in London, Gandhi first began to take a serious interest in religion. There had been a time in his life when he had been sceptical about its value because it did not seem to answer any of the important questions, though he had kept quiet about his doubts because he did not want to upset his parents. The Gandhi household was religious, but in a broad-minded and tolerant way. His father used to discuss religious questions with Muslim and Parsee friends. It was this atmosphere that encouraged Gandhi to develop an enquiring mind.

About Hinduism, his own religion, Gandhi knew very little. When he came to England, he had not even read the Baghavad Gita — the most sacred of the Hindu scriptures. Even at this time he read it only in English, not in the original Sanskrit. Later, in South Africa, he learnt all seven hundred verses off by heart, gradually committing them to memory while he washed and shaved each morning.

Through his study of the Gita, Gandhi first began to develop his ideas on detachment from material possessions — how to attain a state of 'desirelessness' as he called it. The Gita also influenced him to become a man of action — a spiritual person, but one who *acts* rather than sits and reflects. Gandhi did not believe that it was necessary to retreat from the world in order to be spiritual.

At the same time he also read other great religious books, notably the Koran and the Bible. He admits that he found the Old Testament boring and never got beyond the Book of Numbers. But he enjoyed the New

17

Testament, and he was especially moved by the Sermon on the Mount, which he found similar to many ideas in the Gita. Christian ideas continued to influence his thinking all his life.

Meanwhile, Gandhi continued to follow his legal studies, which he never found very demanding. He had enrolled as a law student in November 1888, and he decided to improve himself still further by sitting voluntarily for the London University Matriculation examination, which he took in chemistry, French and Latin. He needed Latin in order to read Roman Law.

He passed his final examinations without difficulty. He was called to the Bar on June 10th 1891 and enrolled in the High Court on June 11th. The following day he sailed for India. It was as if he had taken all he wanted from England and had no wish even to spend another day there.

Gandhi had changed a great deal during his three years in England. He had successfully lived on his own, away from his family, and he had mixed with a wide variety of English people. His new found ideas on diet and religion had begun to shape his thinking, and were to prove more enduring and more important than his formal qualifications, for which he had come to England in the first place. And in a short time he would get the opportunity to put some of these ideas to the test.

5
A Taste of Prejudice

When Gandhi landed in Bombay, his eldest brother Laxmidas was there to meet him. Laxmidas had some bad news for him: Putlibai was dead. She had died while Gandhi was in England, but the family had decided to keep the news from him so as not to upset him while he was studying.

Gandhi's most pressing problem now was to earn some money. He had a wife and family to support, and Laxmidas too expected some return for the money he had provided for Gandhi's stay in England.

Gandhi felt that he could not hope to compete with the local lawyers in Rajkot, who were well versed in Indian law. He decided, therefore, to try his luck in Bombay, where there were plenty of big businesses and more scope for English-trained lawyers. He would also be able to find out more about the day-to-day workings of the Indian courts.

But there was plenty of competition for legal work and it was not easy to get a case. Most lawyers — even the well-established barristers — got their cases by paying touts, who waited around the courts looking for business. Gandhi was disgusted by this and resolved not to get a case in this way. After months of haunting the courts, he finally got the chance to defend a poor woman in the Small Causes court. But when he stood up to speak, he had an attack of nerves and was unable to say a word. He handed the case over to another lawyer and slipped out of the courtroom.

It was a quick end to Gandhi's legal career in Bombay and, after toying with the idea of taking a job

19

as a schoolteacher (for which, however, he did not have the right qualifications), he decided to go back to Rajkot. There he gradually began to establish himself by writing briefs and to earn some money at last. And, but for two chance events, he might have continued in this way.

First his brother asked him to intervene on his behalf with the British Political Agent, who acted as adviser to the ruler of Porbandar. Gandhi had got to know the agent in London. However, he did not think he knew the man well enough to ask any favours, and in any case was not convinced that it was right to ask. His intuition was right. The agent refused to listen and, when Gandhi persisted, ordered the office attendant to throw him out.

This arrogant behaviour on the part of an Englishman came as a shock to Gandhi after he had mixed freely with them for a number of years in England. 'It changed the course of my life', he wrote later in his auto-biography. And now that he had fallen foul of the political adviser, it meant that he stood little chance of ever getting a government post.

The second event was when he was offered a job shortly afterwards. A firm of Muslim businessmen, Dada Abdulla and Company, wanted an Indian lawyer to act on their behalf in South Africa. The fee, £105 for a year's work, all expenses paid, was not magnificent. But Gandhi was now anxious to get away from India, where he felt that he had no future. So, barely a year after he had returned home, he was on his way again, leaving his wife and children behind in Rajkot.

Gandhi had no special ambitions in South Africa except to try his luck and perhaps make a bit of money, like other Indians. He knew little or nothing about the country he was going to and he was totally unprepared for the social and political problems which he encount-ered as soon as he arrived.

South Africa was at that time divided between the

Boers and the British. The Boers, who had settled there from Holland in the sixteenth century, were mostly farmers. They were conservative and deeply religious. The Boers had gradually been pushed inland into the Transvaal and the Orange Free State by the British, who occupied the coastal areas of Cape Colony and Natal.

Both British and Boers led pleasant privileged lives. They owned most of the farms, the businesses and the hotels. They had large houses with beautiful gardens. And they also had plenty of black servants to look after them.

The blacks did all the hard work — on the farms and down the mines. They were supported by the cheap labour force which the British had begun to bring across from India in the early eighteen-sixties.

Other Indians, traders and professional men like Gandhi himself, also came to South Africa to make money. Some succeeded in becoming very rich. But, in the eyes of the white settlers, the British and the Boers, Indians were 'coloured' — just like the black people they employed to work in their houses and on their farms.

It did not take Gandhi long to find this out for himself. After a short spell in Durban with his new employer, who explained his job to him — Dada Abdulla had lent a relative a large sum of money which he was now trying to recover — Gandhi was sent to Pretoria to begin his legal work. He decided to go by train.

As a barrister, trained in England and therefore a person of some importance, Gandhi thought it only right that he should travel first class. All went well for the initial part of the journey, when he was alone in his first class compartment. But at Maritzburg, the capital of Natal, a white man came in. He stared at Gandhi; then went off without saying a word.

When he came back, he had two railway officials with him.

"I'm afraid you can't stay in this compartment," one of the officials informed Gandhi. "You'll have to move to third class."

"But I've got a first class ticket," Gandhi objected.

"It doesn't matter," the offical answered. "Only white people are allowed to travel first class. If you don't leave, I'll have to call a policeman."

"Call one!" was Gandhi's reply.

. The railway official went off and came back with a policeman. Gandhi still refused to move, so the policeman pulled him out of the compartment. Then, still resisting, he was thrown off the train.

Gandhi spent the night in the station waiting room. Maritzburg is high up in the mountains and it was an extremely cold night. His overcoat was locked up in his luggage and he was afraid to ask for it in case he was insulted again. Unable to sleep because of the cold, Gandhi brooded on his experiences on the train.

In India, Indians were often badly treated by the British. Gandhi himself had suffered at the hands of the Political Agent. But the situation in South Africa was far, far worse.

Here he was, a professional man, smartly dressed — and yet he was not allowed to travel in a first class compartment because he was 'coloured'. In South Africa he was no different from the thousands of other poor *coolies* who had come across from India to work in the fields and in the mines.

For the first time in his life, Gandhi had come face to face with colour prejudice. He debated whether to go back to India at once . . . or to get on with his work in Pretoria . . . or to stay and fight this 'deep disease'. He decided to stay and fight.

So, as he sat and brooded in the cold station waiting room at Maritzburg, the transformation of the timid and insecure young man into a politician and social reformer began.

22

6
The Struggle Begins

By the time he reached Pretoria, Gandhi had had further unpleasant experiences at the hands of white South Africans. Other Indians he talked to, there and in Maritzburg, had had similar ones, but they had learnt to live with them. After all, they argued, South Africa was not their country. They had come there to make money and, provided that they were allowed to do that, what did it matter if they had to put up with a few indignities?

Gandhi, still smarting from his humiliating journey, did not share this point of view.

Soon after he arrived in Pretoria, he invited the Indian residents there to a meeting. It was the first time he had spoken in public since his disastrous appearance in the Bombay courtroom, but on this occasion he did not feel at all nervous. He addressed the gathering with quiet confidence.

He began by speaking about his experiences on the journey. His audience nodded: they knew all about things like these.

"But," Gandhi went on, "how can you expect things to change while you behave as you do now? You are always quarrelling amongst yourselves. This really ought to stop. You must learn to get on with one another. It doesn't matter what religion you are — Hindu, Muslim or Parsee — or what part of India you come from. The important thing is that you are all Indians!"

"Besides," Gandhi went on, "Indians have a bad reputation here in South Africa." This made his

23

audience sit up. "People say that Indians cheat. People think that Indians are dirty. This has got to change too! And, if you intend to stay in South Africa, you should all learn English!"

Gandhi even offered to teach them English. Only three young men took up his offer — a barber, a clerk and a shopkeeper. In nine months, he records, two of them at least had learnt enough English for the purpose of their work.

Gandhi held many more meetings during the year he was in Pretoria. The Indians came and listened to him. No one had ever spoken to them so bluntly as this newly-arrived twenty-two year old lawyer. But they took notice. By the end of the year, the Indian residents of Pretoria had formed, with Gandhi's help, their own association.

Meanwhile, Gandhi successfully completed the legal assignment that had brought him to South Africa in the first place. He discovered that the case had been dragging on for years. The lawyers on both sides had been getting richer, but there was still no sign of a settlement.

It seemed to Gandhi that all this legal wrangling in court was hardly in the interests of his client. In the end he persuaded both parties to settle out of court. The arbitrator decided in Abdulla's favour. Gandhi then persuaded Abdulla to allow the debt to be repaid over a number of years so that his relative would not be ruined.

This way of resolving legal disputes, through negotiation rather than litigation, was an approach which Gandhi made a good deal of use of when he later came to practise as a lawyer. "I lost nothing," he observed in his autobiography, "not even money. Certainly not my soul."

Gandhi had every intention of returning to India at the end of the period of his contract. But quite by chance, at a farewell dinner given by his employer in Durban, he was shown a newspaper report about a bill that would take voting rights away from Indians in Natal.

The Indians seemed indifferent to it: only a handful of them were rich enough to vote, anyway.

"We can only understand things that affect our trade," remarked Dada Abdullah.

Patiently Gandhi explained the implications of the bill. "It is the first nail in our coffin," he concluded. The Indians were finally persuaded . . . but then, who could help them — except Gandhi?

Gandhi agreed to stay on for a month in order to fight the bill, and the farewell party was at once transformed into a working committee. It was decided that the main attack on the bill should be through a series of petitions. The first petition, with five hundred signatures, did not succeed in preventing the bill from being passed in Natal. The second, backed up by ten thousand signatures, was sent to London, where the bill had to be approved before it could become law.

In London, the bill was vetoed on the grounds that it discriminated against the citizens of the British Empire. But that was the extent to which the British were prepared to interfere: they did not want to upset the South Africans, on whom they depended for trade. Eventually the bill did get passed, but in an amended form which avoided any explicit racial discrimination.

But the problems that the Indians were facing in South Africa went far beyond this particular piece of legislation. It was soon clear to Gandhi that he would need much longer than a month in order to achieve anything worthwhile — and the Indians were not slow to remind him that he had been the one to advocate action.

But he had to earn money and, since he refused to take any payment for his public work, a number of rich Indians guaranteed him sufficient money to cover his living expenses. He began to work in court and in a

25

short time he was well on the way to establishing himself as a successful advocate.

Gandhi's first move was to organise the Indians in Natal into a political party. He called this the Natal Congress Party, after the Congress Party that already existed in India. But there was a great difference between the two parties. At that time, the Indian Congress Party was rather like a debating society for upper class Indian intellectuals: there was a lot of talk but very little action. The Natal Congress Party, on the other hand, with Gandhi as the driving force behind it, was both socially and politically active.

Gandhi demanded more than nominal support from the people who signed his protests and petitions: they had to understand and believe in what they had signed, not just put their names on a bit of paper. And from the rich he also demanded an appropriate financial commitment — and he had unorthodox ways, verging on blackmail, of making people pay.

Once, for example, a rich man gave a dinner party in his honour. It was a big affair, with a large number of guests. The man probably wanted to impress Gandhi. But Gandhi's main concern that evening was to get his host to double his subscription to the Natal Congress Party. The man refused: he was ready to spend lavishly on entertainment, but not on politics.

Gandhi was determined to get his own way because this man would serve as an example to others: if *he* gave generously, others would follow suit. So he declined to eat anything until the man paid up, and since he was the guest of honour, no one else could eat either. The guests got hungrier and hungrier as Gandhi passed the time talking. Finally, as daybreak came, their host agreed to pay the extra money — and everyone was able to eat.

Signing petitions and joining the Natal Congress Party helped to bring Indians closer together. Gandhi worked hard to cut across religious barriers — Hindu,

26

Muslim, Parsee and Christian — and at the same time to get the rich Indian merchants to recognise that the poor Indian labourers were part of the same community.

Gandhi's first real contact with the labourers was when one of them appeared in his office, bleeding and weeping, his clothes all torn. The man was called Balasundaram and he had been beaten up by his employer. Gandhi had the man treated by a doctor and then successfully arranged for him to be transferred to another employer. As a result, he soon became known as the poor labourers' friend and increasingly they came to him for help.

᳙ The British had been bringing these labourers across from India since 1860, to serve as a cheap work force. Their terms of employment were harsh. They had to work for the same employer for a period of five years, in return for food, lodging and a minimal wage. At the end of this period they could either return to India, passage paid, or else stay on in South Africa on their own account. Many of the labourers elected to do this and some, being hard-working and frugal, became moderately successful.

But, as the Indian population in Natal increased, the whites, expecially the poorer members of the community, began to feel threatened. In 1894 new regulations were introduced. The labourers were offered two main options: either go home after five years or sign on for a second term with the same employer. If they still wanted to work independently, they would have to pay a tax of £3 for every member of the family. This tax was designed to be crippling: £3 was about half of what a labourer could expect to earn in a year.

There were many other restrictions intended both to limit and humiliate the Indian community in South Africa — these 'semi-barbarous Asiatics' as they were described on the statute-books. In Natal, for instance, they had to carry passes if they went out after nine in

27

the evening, otherwise they were liable to be arrested. In the Orange Free State they were not allowed to own property or shops or farms. In Transvaal they had to pay a residence tax every year. In some towns in Cape Colony they were not allowed to walk on the pavement. Gandhi himself was once pushed into the gutter for doing this.

And everywhere the term 'coolie' — a word of contempt for the labourers — was used to describe Indians. There were 'coolie' shopkeepers, 'coolie' teachers — and even 'coolie' barristers like Gandhi himself!

Gandhi did not hope to solve all these problems. He knew that you could not simply sweep away prejudice overnight. But he was determined to stop prejudice from becoming legalised and to establish the principle that Indians, as citizens of the British Empire, were entitled to equality before the law.

For three years he crusaded endlessly for the rights of Indians. He used every possible means to bring the problems of the Indian community to the attention of the public: lectures, meetings, petitions, pamphlets and an endless stream of letters to the press. But he realised that he needed still more time, so in 1896 he went back to India to fetch his wife and family.

7

Satyagraha
The Fight against Repression

Gandhi stayed six months in India. Much of the time he spent publicising the problems of the Indians in South Africa. He wrote a pamphlet on the subject, which sold out almost immediately; he addressed public meetings all over the country, and he enlisted the support of prominent Indian politicians. Then he was summoned back to Natal.

News of Gandhi's speeches travelled ahead of him and, not surprisingly, they had been distorted and misrepresented in the popular press. His return also coincided with the arrival at Durban of a boatload of several hundred Indian immigrants and the rumour soon spread around that Gandhi was planning to flood South Africa with poor Indians!

Determined attempts were made to stop Gandhi and his fellow Indians from landing. There were angry demonstrations on the quayside as well as immigration delays. When permission to land was finally given, Gandhi was advised to go ashore secretly. He refused, although he did send his wife and children ahead.

When Gandhi himself landed, he was quickly identified and mobbed by an angry crowd, who were quite prepared to lynch him. He owed his rescue to the wife of the police chief, who drove off his attackers and took him to the house where his family were staying. The mob followed him there and were only prevented from burning down the house by the police chief himself, who joined in the song that the crowd had made up.

> Hang old Gandhi
> On the sour-apple tree!

When the news of this violence reached London, instructions were sent to prosecute his attackers. Gandhi refused to co-operate — he preferred to forgive and forget — and won a good deal of approval for his generosity. But he pressed ahead with his fight for Indian rights, and kept up the struggle until war broke out between the British and the Boers in 1899.

Gandhi supported the British in their fight against the Boers, which ended with the British annexing the Boer provinces of Transvaal and the Orange Free State. He maintained that, since the Indians based their claim to equal rights on being citizens of the British Empire, they had to support the empire in time of war. It was a patriotic argument that did not appeal to some members of the Indian community, who would have preferred to be conscientious objectors. Gandhi disagreed: a person could not decide to be a conscientious objector just for convenience, he argued.

The Indian contribution to the war effort took the form of ambulance work. Gandhi organised a corps of 1100 volunteers, many of whom were the very labourers who had suffered British oppression. The volunteers often carried out their duties in the front line and under heavy fire, and many were later decorated for their bravery.

Gandhi decided that the end of the war was the right moment to return to India. There was still plenty of work to do in South Africa, but he had co-workers who could carry on and, besides, he expected the British to reward the Indian community for their support during the war.

In 1901, therefore, he went back to Bombay, where he set up a law practice and settled into a comfortable house in the suburbs. He began to attend Congress meetings and to meet the politicians. He also embarked on a tour of India, where he had not lived for any length of time since he was a boy.

He went everywhere by train, always third class, to familiarise himself with some of the problems of his country. The conditions he experienced during this time left him convinced that both the authorities and the poor in India needed to be educated.

Within a year, however, he received an urgent call to go back to South Africa. Far from improving, the conditions for Indians had actually got worse. And Gandhi could hardly refuse to return since he had pledged himself to go if his help was needed.

But he did not expect to have to stay long. In fact, he hoped to resolve most of the problems when he met the Colonial Secretary, who had come out on a visit from England. The Colonial Secretary, however, had little time to spare for Gandhi and the problems of the Indian community, and he had no wish to upset the Boers by interfering in South African affairs.

Gandhi then realised that he was going to be involved in another long struggle. This time it would be mainly in the former Boer province of Transvaal, where many Indians, who had become refugees during the war, were having difficulty getting permission to go back. Gandhi decided to establish himself in the capital, Johannesburg, where he set up a legal practice.

Essentially all Gandhi was asking for was the right for Indians to co-exist.

"We don't want political power," he tried to explain. "All we want is to live side by side with other British subjects in peace."

But the whites, especially the poor whites, were becoming increasingly afraid that the Indians would flood the Transvaal. It was useless to argue that the population figures did not support this and that this fear was groundless. As a first step towards restricting

Indian immigration, all Indian citizens were required to register. Then, in 1906, a new bill was proposed: Indians would not only have to register but also put their fingerprints on a registration form, to be carried around and produced whenever it was called for.

The purpose of the act, it seemed, was to humiliate Indians at all social levels of the community. It put them on the same level as common criminals!

Gandhi began to organise opposition to the bill and a big meeting was held in the Empire Theatre in Johannesburg to discuss it. The building was packed. Feelings ran high and everyone was in favour of resisting. One speaker swore that, with God as his witness, he would never register. Gandhi was delighted with the response, but he was concerned that everyone should understand the implications of such a commitment: it could mean prison, or physical punishment or even death.

In spite of Gandhi's warnings, the meeting ended with everyone present resolving to resist the bill if it became law.

At this stage, probably, no one — not even Gandhi himself — had any clear idea of how they would resist the registration bill. Even a name for the struggle had yet to be coined. The one finally agreed on was *satyagraha*, or firmness in truth. But what form this *satyagraha* would take had still to be worked out in action.

The Registration Act became law in 1907, and all Indians were required to register within thirty days. Opposition was organised through *Indian Opinion*, a journal which Gandhi had helped to establish in 1903. Indians were instructed not to go to the permit offices, which had been set up for the purpose of registration.

The call not to register was a great success: only about five hundred Indians in all turned up at the permit offices. The government was therefore forced to take action. Gandhi and one hundred and fifty others were arrested and sent to gaol.

But this was clearly not a permanent solution, so the politicians had to work out another approach. While he was in prison, Gandhi was invited to meet General Smuts, a former Boer leader who had now become one of the leading politicians. Smuts promised Gandhi that, if Indians registered voluntarily, the government would repeal the act.

Many Indians doubted the sincerity of the government when they were told this. but Gandhi maintained that they had to trust Smuts. He registered, and other Indians followed his example. But still the law was not repealed, and the Indians were caught in the trap which the politicians had set for them. Gandhi was even accused of having been bribed.

Gandhi's reply to the government was simple but effective: he called upon the Indians to make a bonfire of their registration certificates.

So the struggle went on. New regulations were introduced and defied. The Indians now aimed to make things difficult for the government by filling all the prisons. Businessmen and other professional people played a prominent part in the movement to get arrested. Some crossed from Natal into Transvaal, which they did not have a permit to enter. Others sold goods on the streets without a licence. Hundreds were arrested and sent to prison. This time they were sentenced to hard labour.

But as the struggle dragged on, support began to show signs of weakening. Gandhi was worried. Even a lightning visit to London failed to improve the situation. Increasingly he became concerned for the families of his *satyagrahis*, many of whom had been in prison for a long time. He had to find somewhere for them to stay.

Some years before, Gandhi had bought a small farm at a place called Phoenix, not far from Durban in Natal. But this was not big enough for all the families

33

and besides, Phoenix was too far away. Luckily a friend came to his rescue. One of his most enthusiastic followers was a rich German architect by the name of Kallenbach, who had come all the way to South Africa to work with him. One day, while he and Gandhi were walking in the countryside about twenty miles outside Johannesburg, they came across a farm which both of them liked. Kallenbach bought the farm and gave it to his Indian friends. Gandhi was thus able to settle all the prisoners' dependants there. He called the settlement *Tolstoi Farm*, after the Russian writer who had influenced his thinking.

For a while, there was an uneasy truce with the South African government. A prominent politician had come on a visit to South Africa and, anxious to make a good impression, Smuts had promised to lift some of the restrictions on Indians and in particular to abolish the tax on the imported labourers. This time it was Gandhi who was sceptical: he had already had experience of Smuts' 'promises'.

The signal for the final stage of the struggle was soon given. Smuts announced that, after all, he could not abolish the tax on the labourers. This in itself was provocation enough. But then, in 1913, the Supreme Court of Cape Colony ruled that only Christian marriages would be recognised as valid in South Africa. In effect, this made all Indian women concubines and all their children illegitimate!

The refusal to abolish the tax had already brought the labourers into the struggle. They were now joined, for the first time, by the women, Kasturbai among them.

The first thing Gandhi did was to send sixteen women volunteers from Natal into Transvaal. Kasturbai was one of these. The women were arrested and put in prison. Shortly afterwards, a party of eleven women were sent from Transvaal into Natal, where they persuaded the Indian miners in the town of Newcastle to go on strike.

This strike was a development that Gandhi had not

anticipated. The miners lived in company huts and, as soon as they went on strike, the mine owners cut off their water and electricity. Gandhi now had two thousand men on his hands — without homes and without jobs. How was he going to feed them all?

He decided to send his 'army' across the border into Transvaal. If they were arrested, his problem would be solved. If they were not arrested, they could live on Tolstoi Farm.

The march into Transvaal lasted several days. The rations were meagre — each person got one and a half pounds of bread and an ounce of sugar per day — but the miners conducted themselves with great discipline. Gandhi himself was arrested three times in the course of the march. The third time he was sent to prison with hard labour.

In Transvaal, the miners were arrested, put on special trains and sent back to Natal. There they were sentenced to work in the mines which they had abandoned — the mines were now declared to be an 'extension' of the prison — and, when they refused to co-operate, they were whipped and beaten. But still they refused to go back down the mines.

The brutal treatment of the labourers led to a further wave of strikes in Natal. At one time there were over fifty thousand Indians on strike and several thousands in prison. Many Indians lost their lives in the struggle.

The repressive behaviour of the South African government soon became world news. The Viceroy of India himself demanded intervention. In the end, Smuts had to agree to set up a Commission of Inquiry.

Smuts and Gandhi then negotiated for weeks until a settlement was finally reached. Most of the points for which the Indians had fought so stubbornly were conceded: the tax on labourers was at last abolished and Indian marriages were once more recognised as legal.

The struggle had been a long one, but Gandhi had won and at last he felt free to leave South Africa.

Altogether it had taken him twenty-one years to achieve his goal.

Gandhi in South Africa 1905

The Great Salt March 1930

Gandhi with millworkers in England 1931

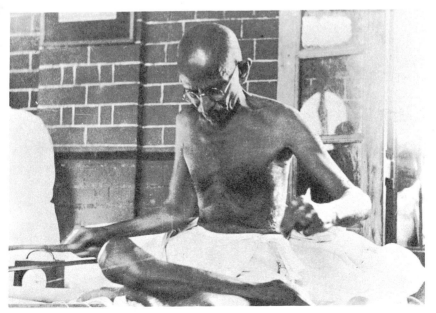

Gandhi spinning

Gandhi with Nehru

Gandhi lying in state

8

The Shaping of Gandhi's Ideas

When Gandhi urged his fellow Indians in South Africa to resist the Registration Act — 'The Black Act', as it later came to be called — he stressed that there must be no violence: the Indians had to fight their oppressors without weapons, even at the risk of death.

This idea, which was not completely new of course, was sometimes called 'passive resistance'. Gandhi, however, did not like this way of describing what he had in mind, mainly because he did not see resistance as something passive.

He decided that a new word must be coined and eventually he settled for the term *satyagraha*. In Sanskrit, *sat* means truth, while *agraha* is firmness. *Satyagraha*, then, is 'firmness in truth' or a kind of 'soul-force'. Gandhi spent the rest of his life developing and refining this concept.

'Real suffering bravely borne melts a heart of stone' he later wrote in his account of the struggle in South Africa. 'Such is the potency of suffering. And therein lies the key to *satyagraha*.'

At a time when anarchists were resisting oppressive governments with murder and other acts of violence, this approach was a significant new weapon, though few people at the time could have imagined that it would be so successful.

Gandhi was not an especially original thinker, nor was he even a great reader. In fact, he had little time for reading except when he was in prison. But the few

37

books he did read made a great impression on him: he had a way of making them part of himself.

Two writers who influenced him in particular were Ruskin and Tolstoi. They came into his life at a time when he was looking around for new ideas with which to re-shape his life. Gandhi, who at one time was earning over £5000 a year, did not want to become just another prosperous lawyer, surrounded by luxuries. You could do without most of these, he decided.

He made a start by washing his own clothes and cutting his own hair. His first efforts naturally caused a great deal of amusement among his colleagues in the law courts, who often used to poke fun at him.

"What's the matter with your hair, Gandhi?" they used to call out. "Have the rats been nibbling at it?"

Gandhi did not mind: he took his hair-cutting seriously. It had started when a white barber had refused to do it for him. Gandhi had been put out at first. Then he began to understand the man's dilemma: the barber's customers were all white.

"If they catch him cutting my hair," he thought, "he'll lose all his regular customers."

Gandhi always tried to appreciate the other person's point of view.

Washing his own clothes, cutting his own hair, running a big house without servants — these were all part of Gandhi's first venture into simple living. But the big revolution came when he was given a copy of Ruskin's *Unto This Last* to read on a long train journey in 1904.

Ruskin, an English Victorian writer and social critic, glorified the simple life based on manual labour. Gandhi sat up all night reading the book. "It was the turning point in my life," he observed later.

Gandhi decided that he had to put Ruskin's principles into practice, which was why he had bought his first farm near Phoenix. There he began his first experiment in community living, with his family, relatives and a number of colleagues.

Living in tents at the start, they had to build their own houses. Everyone had to help to grow food, work in the fields and help in the kitchen. *Indian Opinion*, the journal which Gandhi ran with the help of two Englishmen, Albert West, a printer, and Henry Polak, a journalist, was printed on Phoenix Farm and everyone had to help with that too. Gandhi himself also kept up his law practice and his public work.

But it was at Tolstoi Farm (named after the Russian writer, Count Leo Tolstoi) that Gandhi first began to organise community living on a scale that later provided a model for the ashrams he established in India. Tolstoi's book *The Kingdom of God is within You*, had been the other great influence on Gandhi's thinking — the two men had even corresponded just before Tolstoi's death.

The farm itself was much larger than Phoenix, with a mixed community that included Hindus, Muslims, Parsees and Christians. As at Phoenix, the colonists had to start by building their own houses. Even children had a quota of manual labour. The men did most of the work in the fields, while the women took charge of the kitchens.

There was a school for the children and for any of the older people who felt inclined to learn. Gandhi and his friend Kallenbach were the teachers. But this venture into education was not a great success. The students were too mixed, both in age and background, and they were generally tired when they came to class in the late afternoon. In the end the school had to be closed down.

The colonists also had to do all their own washing and to make their own clothes and shoes. Working with leather, a job traditionally done by untouchables in India, was in itself a revolutionary idea. Gandhi was also very strict about hygiene and made everyone responsible for cleaning out their own lavatories.

"People often get sick because their houses are dirty," he used to say. At Tolstoi he reduced illness to a minimum. "We never had to call a doctor or use drugs," he was later able to boast.

Gandhi was equally strict about diet, which was of course vegetarian. Meat, eggs and fish were not allowed on the farm. Nor was alcohol, coffee or tea. Smoking was also forbidden. These were all rules with which Gandhi later regulated ashram life in India.

All meals on Tolstoi Farm were light, but for Gandhi himself they were lighter still. At the time he was very much under the influence of Kallenbach, who held very extreme views on diet. Kallenbach had even questioned whether food needed to be cooked.

Gandhi, always ready to experiment with new forms of diet, had been easily persuaded and began to live mainly on fruit and nuts. When he discovered that farmers in India had a cruel way of extracting the last drop of milk from the cow's udder, he even took a vow not to drink any more milk.

Gandhi had already adopted the habit of fasting regularly, sometimes for a week at a time. It caused him a great deal of discomfort, especially when he was trying to resume a normal way of life afterwards. He suffered — but he believed that 'all self-denial is good for the soul'.

Gandhi often imposed his ideas on his own family and Kasturbai was forced to go along with them. She accepted his ideas about bringing up the children. They now had four sons whom he taught himself whenever he had time, refusing to send them to regular schools in the belief that character formation was more important than normal education.

She accepted his nature cures rather than the medicines that doctors prescribed, even though there were times when she and the children were at risk.

She accepted too, in 1906, his decision to end their sexual life. Her own fragile health may have been one of the factors, but the fundamental one which influenced Gandhi was the need to be free of physical ties.

40

Brahmacharya, or celibacy, is deep-rooted in Indian thinking.

But in the early days of her stay in South Africa, Kasturbai found it hard to accept the austere way of life that her husband laid down for her and the children, especially as they now had plenty of money and she could reasonably expect a life-style to match her husband's status.

Instead, she was asked to run a large house without the help of servants. The house was always full of visitors, friends and colleagues, some of whom lived there all the time. Kasturbai was expected to do her share of the cleaning, which included emptying the chamber-pots. When she was asked to do this for low caste guests, she revolted.

"Keep your house to yourself and let me go!" she shouted.

"If you don't like it, leave!" Gandhi told her, dragging her to the gate and trying to push her into the street. In those days he had a temper that he had not yet learnt to control. Only Kasturbai's tears, and her pathetic "Where shall I go? I have no parents or relatives here to harbour me" brought Gandhi to his senses.

Again, when they left South Africa in 1901, people gave them lots of expensive presents. Gandhi refused to accept anything for himself and gave his share to help set up a fund for the Natal Congress Party.

But some of the presents were for Kasturbai — and she wanted to keep hers. Unlike most other Hindu women, she had no nice ornaments, Besides, she wanted some jewellery to give her daughters-in-law when her sons got married.

But Gandhi was adamant. "Wasn't this necklace given you for my service?" he demanded.

"And don't I spend my life serving you?" retorted Kasturbai.

But in the end Kasturbai gave way and handed over her share of the jewellery. Deep inside, however, she

41

did not agree with her husband. It was her own private form of 'passive resistance'.

In later years Gandhi admitted that he had learned a good deal about 'passive resistance' from 'Ba'.

9

An Ashram Home

Gandhi was forty-five when he arrived back in India in 1915. He was given an enthusiastic welcome both when he landed in Bombay and later when he visited South India, where most of the poor labourers he had helped in South Africa had come from.

But, although his work in South Africa was well known, he was not politically established and, since he had worked abroad for most of his adult life, he hardly knew his own country or understood its problems.

The leader of the Indian Congress Party at that time was Gopal Krishna Gokhale, who had visited and toured South Africa in 1912. Gokhale had known Gandhi for years and was very impressed by him both as an individual and for his work in South Africa.

"He has a marvellous spiritual power to turn ordinary men into heroes and martyrs," he once observed about Gandhi.

But the political scene in South Africa was very different from India, and Gokhale was worried in case Gandhi should throw himself into politics too quickly and perhaps try out some of the methods he had worked out in South Africa. A few years before, Gandhi had written a small book called *Indian Home Rule*, which even Gokhale had called 'crude and hastily conceived'.

"Spend the first year with your ears open but your mouth shut," he now advised Gandhi. He also suggested that he should travel around India, getting to know the people and their problems. Then, perhaps, he would be in a position to help.

Gokhale had high hopes for the younger man. He was especially keen that Gandhi should join the 'Friends of India Society', which was a select band of workers dedicated to the welfare of their country. Gandhi too was anxious to join — he had a great admiration for Gokhale — but some of the members were against him. They distrusted his use of *satyagraha* as a political weapon and were not attracted by his views on modern science and machinery.

Gokhale died before he could persuade his fellow members of the society to let Gandhi join them. Thus Gandhi lost his 'pilot' right at the beginning of his political career, just as he was about to embark on the 'stormy sea of Indian public life'.

Meanwhile, following Gokhale's advice, he set off on a series of long journeys around India. He travelled everywhere by train, always third class, and often in compartments that were crowded and dirty. He saw a lot of things about India that he did not like, especially the dirt and disease. But he learnt a lot too.

One of the most important things that came home to him during this time was that India was a land of villages — six hundred thousand of them. He soon saw that these and the people who lived in them were the *real* India. This concern for the villages and rural life stayed with Gandhi all his life and was fundamental in shaping his approach to Indian politics.

Early on in his travels, Gandhi visited Rabindranath Tagore, the famous Indian poet and philosopher who had won the Nobel prize for literature in 1913 and had set up his own school at Shantiniketan in West Bengal. Tagore and Gandhi came from very different backgrounds and had very different temperaments (Tagore was aristocratic, intellectual and artistic), but they both shared the same high ideals and had a great admiration for each other. It was Tagore who had first called Gandhi *mahatma* or 'great soul'. "Great soul in beggar's garb" was how he described him.

At Shantiniketan, Tagore had looked after Gandhi's *satyagrahis* on their return from South Africa. Gandhi was now looking for somewhere to house them permanently. He had decided that the place should be Gujarat and he had already discussed the idea with Gokhale, who had promised his support. At the end of his long journey round India, Gandhi stopped in Ahmedabad, which was not far from his own part of the country.

Ahmedabad, the most important city in Gujarat, was rich, prosperous and heavily industrial. It was the centre of the textile industry, with huge mills full of modern machinery that Gandhi so often attacked.

Gandhi was often questioned about his apparently contradictory attitude towards machines. He was not, he used to maintain, opposed to machines in themselves.

"How can I be?" he would say. "My body is a machine. This *charka* (referring to the spinning wheel that he constantly kept by him) is also a machine."

What Gandhi objected to was 'the craze for modern machinery', the use of machines that robbed human beings of their dignity and, in the end, even their means of earning a living.

It was ironic that it was the rich millowners themselves who first came forward with the support that Gandhi needed — he was no longer a rich lawyer and Gokhale had died before he could help — in order to start his first experiment in communal living in India.

Gandhi was delighted. He quickly found a house, where he settled his family and his young followers who had been staying at Shantiniketan. They had already lived together on Tolstoi Farm and understood the routine and discipline of ashram life, based on the principles of *brahmacharya* (celibacy), *ahimsa* (non-violence) and *satya* (truth).

Everything went well at the start. Then one day Gandhi got a letter from a poor schoolteacher called Duda. Duda wanted to come and live in the ashram together with his wife and family.

There was one problem: Duda was an untouchable. Untouchables and caste Hindus did not live in the same part of town, let alone in the same house! They even got their water from separate wells.

Gandhi consulted his fellow ashramites.

"Shall we admit Duda?" he asked.

Gandhi's own views were well known, but he wanted their consent too. They gave it. It was agreed that the ashram was open to anyone who was prepared to accept its rules and discipline. Untouchables were no different from other people. Therefore Duda and his family must be allowed to join them.

But trouble soon broke out. It started with the owner of the house, who used to abuse Duda every time he tried to draw water from the communal well.

"Don't take any notice," Gandhi told Duda. "He'll soon stop bothering you."

Gandhi was right, but this was not the end of the matter. The news got around that untouchables were living in the ashram, under the same roof as caste Hindus. The townspeople were furious. It was immoral, against the Hindu religion! Angry crowds surrounded the house, shouting insults and hurling stones. But still Gandhi refused to send Duda and his family away.

Then the millowners, alarmed by public reaction, decided to withdraw their financial support. But, even more disturbing, Gandhi discovered that some of the people in the ashram — Kasturbai among them — had been stirring up trouble against Duda.

"I'll go and live among the untouchables myself," he threatened. He even adopted Lakshmi, Duda's daughter, so that technically Kasturbai became the mother of an untouchable!

But without money the ashram was in danger of collapse. Help came only at the last moment. One day a stranger, a rich millowner whom Gandhi had met only once before, arrived at the ashram gates. He sat outside in his car and Gandhi had to go out of the house to meet him.

"I hear you need money," the stranger said. Gandhi nodded. "Well, I am prepared to help you — provided you promise not to tell anyone."

Gandhi agreed. It was only much later that the identity of his benefactor was revealed. He was Ambalal Sarabhai, one of the biggest millowners in Ahmedabad.

The next day, the stranger came back with thirteen thousand rupees in banknotes. This was a very large sum of money — enough to enable Gandhi to buy a piece of land on the banks of the River Sabarmati just outside Ahmedabad.

It was a good place for an ashram — and not too far from the prison, either.

"Well, at least I won't have too far to walk!" Gandhi used to joke.

He had, after all, spent quite a lot of time in prison in South Africa and he expected to do the same in India too.

The ashram on the banks of the Sabarmati was to be Gandhi's home for the next sixteen years. It was a place he could retreat to when he wanted to escape from politics or when he needed to rest after one of his long journeys round India.

It was also the place where he was building up and training his *satyagrahis*, the select band of followers who would be needed in the struggle ahead.

10

The People's Helper

Away from the ashram, Gandhi was kept busy with important meetings in various parts of the country. But he was still far from established politically. He also refused to join the Home Rule League, which had been set up in 1915 to agitate for self-government, on the grounds that it was wrong to harass the British while they had a war on their hands. He was also unpredictable. At one big public meeting in Benares, which was attended by a wide range of important people, Gandhi attacked many aspects of Indian life — until he was told to shut up and sit down.

Amongst the masses, however, his reputation was steadily growing. He was already known as the champion of the labourers in South Africa and increasingly ordinary people were coming to him for help and advice.

The first big occasion was at the Indian National Congress, which met in Lucknow in 1916. A peasant by the name of Rajkumar Shukla tried to persuade Gandhi to go with him to Champaran, at the foothills of the Himalayas in Bihar, where a dispute had broken out between the peasants and their landlords. Gandhi was busy at the time and in any case had scarcely heard of Champaran But Shukla refused to take 'no' for an answer. He followed Gandhi back to the ashram and waited until Gandhi gave him a date on which he would come.

For years the peasants on the big estates in the Champaran district, most of which were owned by the British, had been obliged to devote a proportion of their land to growing indigo, which they then handed over as rent. But with the invention of synthetic dyes, the indigo market had collapsed. The landlords said nothing about this and quietly got the peasants to pay to be released from their contracts. When the peasants found out about this, they felt cheated.

When Gandhi finally got to Champaran early in 1917, he lost no time in investigating the peasants' complaints. Almost immediately, however, he was told by the British Commissioner to leave the district by the next train. He refused — and was arrested. Crowds of peasants, who had heard that a *mahatma* had come to help them, turned up at the courthouse where the case was going to be held. Gandhi alone was able to keep them under control. The magistrate in charge of the case had no idea how to proceed and to give himself time, adjourned the case for two hours. Gandhi refused to give bail and was released. Subsequently, on instructions from the government in Delhi, the case against him was dropped and he was allowed to continue with his investigations.

Gandhi had already learnt in South Africa that the law courts were not the best place to settle disputes: they merely dragged out proceedings and put money into the pockets of the lawyers. This had already happened in Champaran, where the lawyers had been taking money from the peasants. Gandhi's approach to the problem was simple but direct: he talked to people; cross-examined them; noted down the facts and drew his conclusions. In the course of the next seven months, he travelled several hundred miles, often on foot, and collected evidence from 8000 peasants.

Meanwhile, the government had appointed a commission of inquiry into the grievances of the peasants. Armed with his formidable body of evidence, Gandhi was able to convince the commission that the landlords were in the wrong and that they had to recompense the peasants. In the end, the amount repaid — twenty-five per cent of the original sum —

49

was small, but in Gandhi's eyes an important principle had been established: landlords, even British landlords, were not all powerful. Even poor peasants had rights. Gandhi had won his first victory in India.

For a while Gandhi stayed on in Bihar, struggling, with the help of fellow workers from the ashram, to try to improve the social conditions of the peasants by setting up schools and hospitals and teaching them to be more hygienic. But then he was called to intervene in another dispute. This time it was on his doorstep in Ahmedabad, where he had his ashram.

A dispute had broken out between the millowners — the same ones who had originally helped to finance his ashram — and the workers, who were asking for higher wages and better working conditions. In Gandhi's view, the workers had a very strong case. It was agreed, however, to set up a commission to arbitrate.

But then, before the commission could start work, the millowners backed out. They offered a 20% increase and threatened to sack any worker who refused to accept it. Gandhi felt that a minimum of 35% was needed, so he advised the workers to go on strike.

It was, however, to be a strike without violence and one that would last until a settlement could be reached.

To make sure that the workers kept to this, Gandhi made them all take a pledge not to return to work until their demands were met. Every day he met and talked to the workers in order to encourage them. After the meetings, the workers paraded through the city carrying banners with the slogan: *Ek Tek!* (Keep the pledge!).

Gandhi's helper in directing the strike was Anasuya Sarabhai, the sister of his mysterious benefactor who had come to his rescue when he needed money for his ashram. Her brother was now on the opposite side.

50

Between them, Gandhi and Anasuya saw that the workers and their families got some food. They also persuaded them to do some useful work such as repairing their huts or cleaning up the settlements where they lived.

But, as the strike dragged on, Gandhi felt that the workers' resolve was weakening. He began to be afraid that they would simply give in and go back to work. Some workers also showed signs of becoming violent. This was something that Gandhi could not allow. It would have been a setback for the cause of *satyagraha*.

Then, at one of their meetings, he heard himself telling the workers that he was going on a fast.

"I will not take any food until we have won," he said.

The words just slipped out of his mouth, but there was no taking them back! Gandhi had often fasted before — but this was the first time he had undertaken one for a public cause.

The workers were stunned. They begged him not to do this for them. They were ready to go on a fast themselves. But Gandhi was adamant. Although he had doubts about the rightness of what he was doing, he could not go back on his word.

After three days, both the millowners and the workers came to the place where Gandhi was publicly fasting, under what had become known as 'Keep the Pledge' tree. Both sides agreed to accept arbitration (and eventually the millworkers got their increase of 35%). But even this was not enough for Gandhi. He also extracted from them a binding agreement to settle all future disputes by arbitration.

Gandhi — almost unintentionally at this stage — had devised a new political weapon for himself. Perhaps on this occasion he may even have misused it. His *intention* had been to make the workers keep their pledge. The *effect* of the fast, however, was to force the millowners to agree to arbitration. It was, therefore, a sort of blackmail.

Gandhi soon had another opportunity to experiment with *satyagraha* when there was trouble in the Kheda district, not far from Ahmedabad. The land in this part of Gujarat belonged to the British government and the peasants who worked on it had to pay taxes in return. Normally, however, if the crops were poor, the taxes were reduced. If the crops failed, the taxes were remitted altogether.

The crops failed in 1918, but the government was in no mood to remit the taxes. The British were at war and needed as much money as they could get.

The peasants sent for Gandhi.

"The law on this point is quite clear," Gandhi told the large meeting that had gathered to hear him. "In circumstances like these you don't have to pay any taxes."

"But what can we do?" the peasants objected. "If we don't pay, the government officials will seize things from our farms and from our houses and sell them to raise money.

Gandhi thought. "Let them seize your things," he said. "But provided nobody buys them, what use will they be to the government? The important thing is that you must all stick together and make sure that nobody buys anything."

Gandhi's advice was enthusiastically received and the peasants refused to pay. Government officials seized the peasants' property — but they had no way of disposing of it. So, in the end, the British had to make some concessions and it was agreed that only the very rich peasants should pay any tax.

The Kheda campaign was only a partial victory for Gandhi. Perhaps he felt that at this stage, with Britain still at war, he had gone as far as he could. But what was important was that, in each of these three struggles — Champaran, Ahmedabad and Kheda — he had demonstrated that *satyagraha* could be an effective weapon.

And it did not take long for news of these moral victories to spread through India.

11

Non Co-operation

Although agitation for home rule increased during the First World War (1914–1918), India had continued to give Britain substantial aid both with money and with men. Hundreds of thousands of Indian troops fought in Europe and in the Middle East; thousands lost their lives. It was natural, therefore, at the end of the war, for Indians to expect some recognition in the form of more effective participation in government.

Instead, it was proposed to continue and to extend many of the wartime restrictions on civil liberties, which included censorship of the press, secret trials and bans on demonstrations. Congress leaders protested, but to no purpose. With the Rowlatt Act of 1919, these restrictions became law.

Gandhi first read about these proposals in the newspaper while he was recovering from an illness that had nearly killed him. Ironically, he had got ill while he was trying, without much success, to recruit soldiers for the British Army in Kheda, where earlier he had led the peasants in a *satyagraha* campaign against taxes. Only careful nursing and a change of diet — Kasturbai persuaded him to drink goat's milk — saved his life.

Gandhi was deeply shocked by the news. Up to this moment he had always been convinced that, even if the British sometimes made mistakes, on the whole their rule was benevolent and in the long run good for India. He regarded himself as a loyal subject of the King Emperor, even taking a public oath of loyalty to the British Empire in 1915.

Gandhi now began to make plans for *satyagraha* on

a national scale, although without any clear idea at the time of what form the action would take. It was only later, during a visit to Madras, that he evolved a plan of action. According to him, it came to him in a dream. And, like many of his schemes, the plan was delightfully simple.

All India must observe a one day *hartal*, or strike. "Everyone in India must stop work for one complete day," he explained. "Shops, offices, factories . . . all must close. Schools, too. And, for twenty-four hours, every Indian must fast and pray."

A national *hartal* was a brilliant idea. It was also Gandhi's first major political act against the British.

The news of the proposed strike soon travelled round India. Gandhi now had lots of supporters all over the country, many of them women (whose help he especially valued, now as in South Africa) and young people, and the idea of non-violent protest was carefully explained to the masses. The day chosen for the *hartal* was March 30, 1919, but this date was later changed to April 6.

But India was not quite ready for an experiment of this kind. In Bombay, where Gandhi himself was present, the day passed off peacefully. But in Delhi and the Punjab the *hartal* was staged early, on the original date, and was accompanied by violence.

When Gandhi heard that riots had broken out in the north, he at once set off by train to try to stop them. But the British were determined to keep him away from the scene and had him taken off the train. The rumour then got around that Gandhi had been arrested, and rioting broke out in Ahmedabad and Bombay. Gandhi was deeply disturbed. This was not *satyagraha*, he told his followers. On April 18 he called the campaign off and, as a penance, went on a seventy-two hour fast.

Gandhi's own verdict was that he had made an error of judgement in asking the Indian people to make a non-violent protest. 'A Himalayan miscalculation', he later called it. The Indian people were not ready yet for civil disobedience, he concluded, because they had not yet had any training in civil obedience.

Meanwhile the disturbances in the north, especially in the Punjab, continued. The British began to take action and arrested two leading political figures. This resulted in further outbreaks of violence in the holy Sikh city of Amritsar, during which a number of British residents were assaulted and murdered.

By now the British authorities were becoming alarmed, thinking that they had the beginnings of a full-scale rebellion, like the Indian mutiny in 1857, on their hands.

A senior British Army officer, Brigadier General Dyer, was despatched to get the situation in Amritsar under control. One of Dyer's first acts was to forbid any further meetings and processions. The proclamation banning these was read aloud throughout the city on April 13.

The following day, Dyer got news that a mass meeting was going to be held in Jallianwalla Bagh, a piece of land in the city surrounded by buildings. It was not clear whether the demonstrators were defying his proclamation or simply had not heard it. Dyer rushed to Jallianwalla Bagh with his troops. There he found thousands of people crammed inside the enclosed space. Dyer immediately ordered his troops to open fire. In a few minutes, over four hundred people lay dead and about fourteen hundred had been wounded. Almost every bullet had found its mark.

At an inquiry that was later held into the massacre, Dyer explained that he wanted to teach the Indians a lesson that they would not forget. In this he succeeded: the Indians did not forget this lesson. Although Dyer was nominally punished and sent back to England for his conduct, the massacre at Jallianwalla Bagh and the humiliations which the people of Amritsar were forced to submit to in the following weeks proved to be a turning-point in Anglo-Indian relations. And for Gandhi too, although he called off his campaign of active civil disobedience, the events in the Punjab, which the British prevented him from investigating for himself, resulted in complete disillusionment with the British government in India.

Reforms and concessions followed in an attempt to make amends, and a power-sharing formula was worked out. Gandhi advised Congress to accept these reforms, but at the same time he felt that there was no turning back in the struggle against the British. He joined the Home Rule League in 1920 and also became its president. He was now a fully-fledged politician and the acknowledged leader of Congress.

For the new stage in the struggle against the British Gandhi devised the slogan 'non co-operation'. This was to take many forms. British imported goods, especially cloth, were to be boycotted. So were British schools, law courts and offices. Peasants were to refuse to pay their taxes. British honours were to be rejected. Gandhi sent back to the Viceroy of India the medals which he had won in South Africa. Many prominent Indian politicians resigned their honours. Tagore sent back his knighthood.

"I can retain neither respect nor affection for a government which has been moving from wrong to wrong, in order to defend its immorality", Tagore said.

The programme for non co-operation was approved at the Nagpur Conference of 1920. For months after this, Gandhi — now very much a *mahatma* against his own wishes — toured the country tirelessly, explaining the purpose of the non co-operation movement, which, he claimed would bring *swaraj*, or home rule, within twelve months.

Everywhere he went he addressed huge audiences. To start with, he explained, in order to be free of foreign rule, Indians must stop wearing clothes made from imported cloth, which was a symbol of foreign domination. Gandhi used to conclude his meetings by asking members of the audience to take off the foreign clothes they were wearing. These were then piled up in a huge heap, which Gandhi himself set light to.

At the same time, Gandhi stressed that everyone should learn to spin and weave. He himself used to do this for half an hour every day. Homespun cloth became an obsession with him. He even simplified his own form of dress, so that he now wore only a kind of loin cloth.

At the start, the British dismissed the non co-operation movement. But its potential began to be appreciated when the Prince of Wales visited India in November 1921. When he drove through the streets of Bombay, he found the city deserted. Shops were closed and the Indian people remained shut up in their houses.

As unrest throughout the country grew, restrictions on civil liberties were once again introduced. By January 1922 thousands of Congress leaders had been arrested and thrown in gaol.

Meanwhile, a new Viceroy, Lord Reading, had been sent out to India. Reading invited Gandhi to come to Delhi to explain his plans and aims. On a personal level he got on well with the Viceroy, but not surprisingly, many of his ideas were unacceptable. Non-violence was all very well as a religious idea, but not as a plan of action designed to drive the British out of India!

On the Indian side, not all members of the Congress Party were satisfied with Gandhi's campaign of non-violent non co-operation. They began to press for more effective action. A resolution was passed to try out civil disobedience campaigns in different parts of the country at the same time. Gandhi himself did not agree with this line of action, perhaps because he was worried that it might get out of hand. So he argued that civil disobedience should be tried out in one part of the country only, as an experiment. The purpose of this would be to see if British administration in that area could be brought to a complete standstill.

The region and date for the experiment were chosen. But, on February 5 1922, just a few days before the campaign was due to start, a tragedy occurred. In Chauri Chaura, a small village in the Himalayas, an angry mob attacked some policemen, who had molested them during a procession. The policemen took refuge inside the town hall, which the mob then set alight. Twenty-two policemen were murdered as they tried to escape from the burning building.

Gandhi was appalled. He went on a personal five day fast to purify himself and called off the civil disobedience campaign. India, he was reluctantly compelled to conclude, was still not ready for independence through non-violent action.

12

The Great Trial

During the civil disobedience campaign Lord Reading had been under pressure from the government in London to arrest Gandhi. The provincial governors in Bombay, Madras and Calcutta also wanted Gandhi out of the way. Only the Viceroy himself held back: he felt that he could not arrest Gandhi unless he committed some concrete act of sedition.

Finally, however, after consultation with the provincial governors, Lord Reading issued the order for Gandhi's arrest on March 1 1922 and, ten days later, Gandhi was taken into custody. A police car was sent to the Sabarmati ashram, where Gandhi had gone to stay. The car stopped some way from the ashram and a policeman was despatched to Gandhi's hut to tell the mahatma that he should consider himself under arrest. Gandhi was given a few minutes to pray and to listen while his favourite hymn was sung by his fellow ashramites. Then he was taken off to the gaol nearby — where he had often joked that he would one day find himself.

The charge on which Gandhi was arrested was the publication of three seditious articles in *Young India*, the journal which he had been bringing out since 1919. The printer and publisher of the journal, Shankarlal Banker, was also arrested and charged.

The case against Gandhi was clear cut. In one of the articles he had written: 'Non co-operation aims at the overthrow of the government and is therefore legally seditious.' In another: 'Non co-operationists are at war with the government. They have declared rebellion against it.'

All the articles had in fact been published some time before Gandhi's arrest and what is surprising, therefore, is that the Viceroy waited so long before taking any action. It appears, however, that after Gandhi called off the civil disobedience campaign, the Viceroy felt that he was a spent force and that his arrest would no longer touch off a wave of riots throughout the country.

Faced with the charges, Gandhi pleaded guilty. He gave his age as fifty-three and his occupation as 'farmer and weaver'.

The trial — 'The Great Trial' as it came to be called (Gandhi was arrested many times in India but brought to trial only once) — opened on March 18 in the Government Circuit House in Ahmedabad. The judge was Mr Justice Broomfield and the prosecutor was the Attorney General of Bombay. Gandhi and Shankarlal Banker offered no defence.

Gandhi began by reading a prepared statement to the court in which he explained how he — who had once been a loyal supporter of the British Empire — had come to rebel against it.

"In South Africa," he said, "I discovered that as a man and as an Indian, I had no rights." But still he thought that the British system was right and good. That was why he had supported the British in their various wars.

Then he described the growth of his disillusionment, starting with the restrictions on civil liberties after the war and referring directly to British behaviour in the Punjab at the time of the Jallianwalla Bagh massacre.

"I came reluctantly to the conclusion," he said, "that the British connection made India more helpless than she ever was before, politically and economically."

The British, he went on, were destroying India. For that reason, he concluded, "I hold it an honour to be disaffected towards a government which has done more harm to India than any previous system."

Gandhi accepted full responsibility for the outbreaks

61

of violence that had occurred, and asked the judge for the highest penalty.

"The only course open to you," he told Justice Broomfield, "is to resign your post . . . or to inflict on me the severest penalty if you believe that the system and law you are assisting to administer are good for the people of this country."

Sentencing Gandhi, Judge Broomfield said: "It will be impossible to ignore the fact that you are in a different category from any person I have ever tried or am likely to try. It would be impossible to ignore the fact that, in the eyes of millions of your countrymen, you are a great leader and patriot."

The judge sentenced Gandhi to six years in prison, adding that he would be pleased if the sentence was reduced. Shankarlal Banker was sentenced to one year.

Gandhi thanked the judge for his light sentence and for his courtesy throughout the trial. Then, after a trial that had lasted only ninety minutes, he was taken off to Yeravda Central Gaol in Poona.

In prison Gandhi was not unhappy. There were some irritating restrictions at the start — he was not allowed to spin, for example — but once these were lifted, he found prison life peaceful and relaxing. He had time to read a great deal. He studied two Indian languages. He also began to write the story of his life.

And, while he was in prison, Gandhi also thought a great deal about India's problems. For the moment, the civil disobedience campaign had failed and home rule had not been achieved in twelve months. Gandhi now set himself to work out a programme which would prepare Indians for independence.

First, they must learn to make their own cloth. "If we make our own cloth," Gandhi argued, "this will provide work for the unemployed poor. Most of these live in villages and work will help the villages to become more important."

Bringing recognition and new life to the villages was one of Gandhi's great dreams.

Next, Hindus and Muslims must learn to live together in peace. India belonged to both of them, Gandhi maintained. Despite their different religious beliefs and their different customs, they had lived together in the past and must work together for independence in the future.

Finally, caste Hindus must help the untouchables. This was perhaps the thorniest problem of all. There was nothing the British could do — no law prohibiting untouchability — that would help. Untouchability was an Indian problem, to which only Indians themselves could find an answer.

Gandhi did not serve the whole of his six year sentence. After two years, he fell seriously ill with appendicitis. Before the operation began, he gave his written consent so that the British would not be blamed if he died. But the operation was a success, in spite of some uneasy moments when the electricity failed and the operation had to be finished by lamplight.

Gandhi was slow to recover from the operation, however, and the British authorities decided to release him. Once again, he was thrust out into the 'turbulent world' of Indian politics.

13

A Pinch of Salt

When Gandhi came out of prison in 1924, he was faced with two major changes in the political situation.

First, a split had developed inside the Congress Party. One faction, which called itself the Swaraj (or Home Rule) Party, advocated working within the councils which had been set up by the British as the administrative framework for their power-sharing policy. They argued that in this way they would gradually be able to undermine the administration from within and thus achieve home rule. The other faction, who had come to be known as the 'No-changers', wanted to continue Gandhi's own policy of non co-operation.

This was a dilemma for Gandhi. He did not favour the approach of the Swaraj Party, but it had a lot of powerful support. One of its leaders was Motilal Nehru, father of the future Prime Minister of India and one of the leading politicians of the time. But his main concern was to prevent the Congress Party — the only effective instrument for achieving Indian independence — from being torn apart. He decided, therefore, to sign a pact with the Swaraj Party and give his approval to their aims.

A second and no less serious problem was that Hindu-Muslim unity had broken down. There had been a time, before Gandhi went to gaol, when Hindus and Muslims worked together for the common cause of home rule and eventual independence. But now both sects had begun to provoke one another again. Riots broke out; Hindus and Muslims killed one another and tension began to rise.

Gandhi, in India as much as in South Africa, had always felt strongly about Hindu-Muslim unity. It was a subject he wrote about a great deal in his journal, *Young India*. He could not understand why Hindus and Muslims should be so intolerant towards one another.

To give publicity to the issue, Gandhi announced a twenty-one day fast, to begin on September 18 1924. This had an immediate effect. A 'Unity Conference' was called in Delhi, which passed resolutions condemning violence and other provocative acts such as compulsory conversion. Gandhi agreed to break his fast. He was satisfied that, for the moment, there was peace between the two communities, although deep down he realised that peace could not last.

For the next three years, Gandhi withdrew from the political scene. His main preoccupation now was with social issues. He travelled extensively throughout India, speaking on problems such as child marriage, untouchability and spinning.

This last topic was his favourite and most constant theme. Increasingly, he saw the production of *khadi* (homespun cloth) as a major solution to the country's economic problems, as a way of providing work and a small income for the millions of unemployed and under-employed in the rural areas.

Gandhi wanted everyone to spin; he also wanted everyone to buy and wear *khadi*. It was particularly important for people who lived in towns to do this: it would be a way of repaying their debt to the peasants on whom they depended.

Gandhi's obsession with spinning (and with the spinning wheel, which was eventually to become the symbol on the flag of independent India) did not appeal to all his fellow Congress-workers, especially the sophisticated ones. But slowly they began to realise that, even if Gandhi exaggerated its importance, the production of *khadi* made economic sense. Homespun cloth became the badge of the Indian nationalist and even the aristocratic Nehrus took to wearing it.

65

In 1927, India got a new Viceroy: Lord Irwin (who later became Lord Halifax). His predecessor in office, Lord Reading, had predicted on his departure that Indian politics would be quiet for about eighteen months. Then it would begin to 'warm up'.

This was exactly as events turned out.

The occasion for the 'warming up' was an announcement by the Viceroy, who summoned key Indian leaders to Delhi to hear it, that a Royal Commission was being set up to review the Indian constitutional position — in effect, to see if India was ready for some form of independence.

The Commission itself was no news (it had been announced in all the papers); but what did disturb and upset the Indian political leaders was that not a single Indian was invited to sit on it. Feeling that they were being excluded from taking part in decisions that affected the life of their own country, they decided to boycott the commission altogether.

Having effectively frustrated the work of the commission, the Indian leaders were then challenged to produce their own ideas for a constitution. Their response, at the Annual Congress Conference in 1928, was to ask for dominion status (like that enjoyed by Canada and Australia) to be given to India within twelve months — otherwise they would demand complete independence.

Gandhi reluctantly supported the resolution. Personally, he would have preferred a longer period of two years. Meanwhile, he pressed ahead with his relentless programme of touring the country: if Indians were to be free, they would need to be educated in the responsibilities of freedom.

Three months before the twelve month period expired, Lord Irwin made his response. He announced a Round Table Conference in London to discuss the future of India. Indian leaders were delighted: at last they seemed to be achieving their goal.

But then, at a meeting between Irwin and Gandhi on

66

December 23, it emerged that the Viceroy could not guarantee that the Round Table Conference would be mainly concerned with drafting a new constitution for India.

This revelation came just before the Annual Congress Conference, which was being held at the end of December 1929. Congress, under the presidency of the forty-year old Jawaharlal Nehru, the future Prime Minister of India, passed a resolution in favour of independence and secession. The flag of the Congress Party — the flag of free India — was also raised for the first time. It was resolved that civil disobedience should start again and it was left to Gandhi to work out how and when.

Gandhi's first move was on January 26 1930, when he called on all Indians to celebrate independence by taking a pledge to support the civil disobedience campaign. The response was favourable — but still Gandhi waited. In fact, he was waiting for inspiration to come to him through what he called his 'inner voice', which had often helped him in the past. And when the idea did finally come to him, it was brilliantly simple, like so many of Gandhi's other ideas in the past.

Gandhi's plan was that Indians must break the Salt Law by making their own salt. Salt was a government monopoly and there was a tax on it. It was a tax that everyone — rich and poor — had to pay because everyone needed salt. But it was an especially unfair tax because it was a much greater burden for the poor.

Gandhi, with real theatrical instinct, announced that he himself would give a signal for breaking the law. He would march from the Sabarmati ashram to the sea together with a select band of *satyagrahis*. There, at a place called Dandi, which was over two hundred miles from Ahmedabad, he would take a pinch of salt from the sea. This would be a signal for the rest of India to begin breaking the law.

But first he wrote a long letter to the Viceroy,

67

warning him that civil disobedience was about to start again and explaining the reasons.

'Dear Friend, . . . ', he began. He then went on to explain that he did not want to hurt the English, but the time had come for India to free herself of their 'curse'. British rule, he wrote, 'has reduced us politically to serfdom. It has sapped the foundations of our culture. It has degraded us spiritually.'

The Viceroy himself did not reply to Gandhi's letter. Instead, he instructed his secretary merely to say that he was sorry that Mr Gandhi was taking a course of action that involved breaking the law.

In fact, the Viceroy did not take Gandhi's scheme very seriously. His advisers had already assured him that any violation of the Salt Law would hardly affect the revenue! Like many of Gandhi's own supporters, the British did not fully appreciate at this stage the implications of what Gandhi proposed to do.

At last, on March 12 1930, the sixty-one year old Gandhi set off with his band of seventy-eight followers on the two hundred and forty mile march to the sea. Each day they walked twelve miles. 'Child's play' was how Gandhi described it. The mahatma was in very good physical condition at the time and he walked so fast that many of his younger followers could not keep up with him.

At night they stopped at one of the villages on the route. Here, as in every place they passed through, Gandhi explained the purpose of the march to the villagers who gathered round to listen to him. He also took advantage of the occasion to address them on his other favourite themes — child marriage, untouchability and spinning. Throughout the march he kept up his own quota of spinning every night as an example to the others. Then he wrote up his diary for the day — a practice which all the marchers had to follow.

When the band came to leave the following morning, many of the villagers joined them. By the time they reached Dandi, Gandhi's original band of seventy-

68

eight followers had grown to several thousands.

They reached Dandi on April 5 and spent the night in prayer. The following morning, Gandhi went into the sea and bathed. Then he returned to the beach and picked up a few grains of salt, which the sea had left on the sand.

It was the signal the nation had been waiting for. All over India people began breaking the Salt Law. Those who lived near the coast went into the sea and made salt. In inland towns and cities, people bought and sold salt that had been made illegally.

The British, who had not taken Gandhi's own act of defiance very seriously, were now forced to act. In the next few months, thousands of Indians were arrested and thrown into gaol. Many prominent Congressmen, Jawaharlal Nehru among them, got themselves arrested by making or selling salt. In the space of a year, over sixty thousand Indians were put in prison.

The police often used violence but, with few exceptions, violence was very rarely used in return. Gandhi, who had now withdrawn from the scene to a place near Dandi — he had vowed not to return to the Sabarmati ashram until the Salt Law had been repealed — must have been satisfied with the progress that the Indian people had made since the massacre at Chauri Chaura.

Soon it was Gandhi's turn to go to prison too. On May 5 a detachment of Indian policemen, together with a British magistrate, was sent to arrest him in the middle of the night. Once again he was ordered to be detained in Yeravda Central Gaol.

This time there was no trial.

14

Gandhi in England

The political situation in India was now causing the British government both concern and embarassment. Congress leaders, including Gandhi and Nehru, were locked up in gaol along with thousands of other Indians — and yet, as Gandhi had predicted from the start, it was becoming increasingly difficult to govern the country.

What was worse, however, was that Britain had lost face in the world. The march on the Dharasana Salt Works, a hundred and fifty miles north of Bombay, had been widely reported in the international press.

In the course of the march hundreds of volunteers, led by Mrs Sarojini Naidu, an Indian poetess who had become one of Gandhi's most fervent supporters, and Manilal Gandhi, the mahatma's second son, were beaten unconscious by the police as they tried to get into the salt works.

'There was no fight, no struggle; the marchers simply walked forward until they were struck down,' was how an American journalist described it.

'England,' said Tagore, in an interview which was published in the *Manchester Guardian*, 'is no longer regarded throughout the world as the champion of fair dealing and the exponent of high principles . . . but as the upholder of Western race supremacy and the exploiter of those outside her own borders.'

Colonialism had been exposed. Britain still ruled India, but the Indians realised that they had already demonstrated their power to become free whenever they wanted.

In this climate the Viceroy still stubbornly insisted that the Round Table Conference should go ahead. He even wanted Congress leaders to attend it. They, naturally, could find no common ground for negotiation with the British, and the conference was held without them.

The Viceroy then decided to release Gandhi and other Congress leaders. Gandhi, always willing to try to find a solution through negotiation, offered to go to Delhi for discussions with Irwin.

The two men, both high principled and deeply religious, got on well together. Their meetings, eight in all, lasted for a total of twenty-four hours. As a result of the talks, Gandhi agreed to call off the civil disobedience campaign and Irwin too made a few concessions.

These meetings did not please everybody. The Conservative politician, Winston Churchill, resented the fact that the Viceroy was having to negotiate with Gandhi as if he were an equal.

"It is nauseating," he said, "to see Mr Gandhi, a seditious Middle Temple lawyer, now posing as a fakir of a type well known in the East, striding half-naked up the steps of the Viceroy's Palace, while he is still organising a defiant campaign of civil disobedience."

Many Indian politicians were displeased with the outcome of the talks. It was felt that Gandhi had given way on too many issues. Nehru in particular was appalled that the question of independence — which Congress had announced as its goal — had been lost sight of altogether.

On his side, Gandhi probably felt that concessions had to be made at this point. After all, the Indians had effectively demonstrated that they were masters in their own country, even if they were not yet independent. He also firmly believed that *satyagraha* did not consist entirely of fighting: there was also a time for negotiating with one's opponent.

71

It was in this spirit that Gandhi agreed to go to London as the sole representative of Congress at the Second Table Conference.

"I will go to London," Gandhi said before he sailed for England at the end of August 1931, "but I shall probably come back with empty hands. The elephant is powerless to think in terms of the ant, in spite of the best intentions in the world, and the Englishman is powerless to think in terms of the Indian."

In one respect Gandhi was right, because the conference itself turned out to be a failure. The delegates who attended it represented too many sections of Indian society and their conflicting interests. The Muslim leader fought on behalf of the Muslims; the Untouchable leader held out for the rights of his community. Only Gandhi claimed to speak for the whole of India.

In the end, more attention was paid to communal issues than to the kind of constitution India would need in order to allow her to enter into a partnership on equal terms with Britain — which was Gandhi's goal.

Gandhi was persuaded to concentrate his efforts as much on the public as on the conference itself, although this absorbed much of his working time. His visit to England was an ideal opportunity to present the Indian point of view to the British people, not all of whom shared Winston Churchill's point of view, and Gandhi was exactly the right man to do it.

Almost overnight, Gandhi was a great personal success in England. The west had never seen a political leader like him and the papers were full of him. 'The Mickey Mouse of India' was the affectionate nickname given to him, because of the way his ears stuck out like those of Mickey Mouse.

While he was in England, Gandhi met and talked to a wide range of figures from public life: politicians such as Lloyd George, the former Prime Minister, and his old adversary, General Smuts; religious leaders such as the Archbishop of Canterbury; teachers like

72

Professor Gilbert Murray; writers like George Bernard Shaw — and actors like Charlie Chaplin.

Gandhi never went to the cinema himself and had not even heard of Charlie Chaplin. He only agreed to meet him when he heard that Chaplin had come from a poor family in the East End, where Gandhi himself had stayed for a time when he first came to England as a student and where he was now staying once again.

Gandhi addressed committees and meetings. He visited schools and universities. He went to the cotton mills in Lancashire, where he was a great success with the unemployed workers, — the same workers whose jobs he had helped to destroy through his campaign against cotton goods imported into India.

While he was in London, Gandhi did not stay in one of the grand hotels in the West End, where the conference was being held in St. James' Palace. Instead, he chose to live in Kingsley Hall, a settlement among the poor in the East End of London, where he had promised a friend he would stay if he ever came to London.

Living in the East End added a great deal to Gandhi's already long working day — by the time he got home and had dealt with his correspondence, he sometimes had only a couple of hours' sleep before he got up again for prayers and his morning walk — but it gained him lots of friends among the poor, with whom he soon became a great favourite. They used to invite him to their houses; they gave parties for him and, when the time came for him to leave England, they gave him lots of farewell presents.

He was a great favourite with the children too and never got tired of answering their questions. They used to tease him a good deal.

"Hey, Gandhi!" one child called out after him. "Where are your trousers?"

This was because Gandhi wore only a loin cloth, like millions of India's poor peasants, instead of conventional Western clothes, which would have given him greater protection against the English winter.

Throughout his visit his dress aroused a great deal of comment.

"You wear plus fours," he once explained, referring to the type of knee length trousers that were in fashion at the time, "I wear minus fours!"

Gandhi always had a quick and witty answer ready.

A loin cloth, shawl and sandals was all Gandhi wore when he went to a tea party which King George the Fifth gave at Buckingham Palace for the delegates to the conference. At first the King had been reluctant to invite the man who had caused so much trouble in India.

"Besides," he objected, "he doesn't even wear proper clothes!"

"It doesn't matter, Your Majesty," he had been told. "He will be cold, not you!"

After the party, someone asked Gandhi if he had been cold at Buckingham Palace.

"How could I be?" Gandhi answered. "The King was wearing enough clothes for both of us!"

The conference in London went on for nearly three months. At the end of it Gandhi returned to India 'empty-handed' — just as he predicted when he left.

"But I have not compromised the honour of my country," he said when he landed at Bombay.

15
Back to Prison

The last thing Gandhi was expecting when he returned from the Round Table Conference was to go back to gaol! And yet this is what happened — and within a week.

Lord Irwin had been replaced as Viceroy by Lord Willingdon, the former Governor of Bombay, and, even while the conference in London was still going on, the new Viceroy was laying plans to render the Congress Party ineffective.

Shortly before Gandhi landed at Bombay, Nehru and another political leader from the Punjab, Abdul Ghaffar Khan (sometimes known as the 'Frontier Gandhi') were arrested. In two major provinces in the north, repressive measures were taken against the Congress Party. These measures included the right to search party premises and the confiscation of funds.

On December 28, the very evening that he landed, Gandhi addressed a huge Bombay crowd.

"I take it that these are Christmas gifts from Lord Willingdon, our Christian Viceroy!" he said as he explained how matters stood. "Something had to be given me — and this is what I have got!"

Deeply concerned by the way events had developed, Gandhi sent a telegram to the Viceroy, asking for an interview. There was no conciliation in the reply that the Viceroy's secretary sent: the Viceroy would be pleased to see Mr Gandhi, but there could be no question of discussing government measures.

Gandhi and the Viceroy continued to exchange telegrams, but the Viceroy held firm in his intention not to negotiate.

"The government has banged the door in my face!" Gandhi exclaimed in the end.

The authorities did more than that: they had him arrested and taken off to Yeravda Prison again. Gandhi had nicknamed the prison 'Yeravda Temple' — because he found peace and time for prayer there.

During the next few months, the Viceroy intensified his repressive measures. Thousands of Indians were arrested. The prisons were as full as they were at the time of the breaking of the Salt Law in 1930. And, to make sure that Gandhi and Congress got no publicity, the press was heavily censored.

Back in prison, Gandhi kept up his usual routine of spinning, prayer and dealing with his heavy correspondence. As during his previous spells of prison life, he did lots of reading and also found time to write a small book. He studied astronomy and used to spend a lot of time watching the night sky to try to understand 'the mysterious universe'.

When he first returned to prison, the authorities tried to make the stay of their distinguished guest as comfortable as possible by providing him with special furniture. When he queried this, he was told that extra money had been allocated for this purpose.

"And where does this money come from?" Gandhi had asked. "I will tell you. It comes out of the taxes which poor Indians have to pay! Take the furniture away. I don't want it!"

He also asked for his living expenses in prison to be kept to about a rupee a day.

Meanwhile, in London, the British government had gone ahead with the task of drafting a new constitution for India, and Gandhi was perturbed to learn that, under the terms of the constitution, Untouchables would be allowed to elect their own representatives to Parliament.

It was an idea that Gandhi had strongly opposed when it was put forward at the Round Table conference by Dr B R Ambedkar, the dynamic leader of the untouchable community. He had virtually had to concede that Muslims should have their own representatives: at least they had a different religion. But Untouchables, he argued, were Hindus: to treat them as a separate community would be to divide India even further.

"I have to resist your decision," Gandhi informed the British Prime Minister. He announced that he would begin a fast on September 20.

The British government was taken aback by this turn of events. Under the terms of the new constitution, some members of the untouchable community would actually enjoy two votes, the first as Hindus and the second as Untouchables. The British had imagined that Gandhi, as the champion of the dowtrodden Untouchables, would approve of this!

Many Indians were also surprised. Some, like Nehru, were irritated because the issue for which Gandhi was now prepared to sacrifice his life seemed to them less important than independence. For Nehru, untouchability was a 'side issue'. It was not until he saw the impact of Gandhi's decision on the country that he began to change his mind.

'Bapu had a curious knack of doing the right thing at the psychological moment,' Nehru observed, describing how he emerged from his crisis on hearing that Gandhi might die, 'and it might be that his action — impossible as it was from my point of view — would lead to great results . . . Then came the news of the tremendous upheaval all over the country . . . What a magician, I thought, was this little man sitting in Yeravda Prison, and how well he knew how to pull the strings that move people's hearts.'

At noon on September 20 1932, Gandhi began his fast — aimed he said, not against the British but 'to sting the Hindu conscience'. At the end of the first twenty-four hours he was already weak. By the fourth day he had high blood pressure and his doctors were seriously concerned for his life. Kasturbai, who had been detained in another prison, was allowed to join him.

"Again, the same story!" she said when she saw him. Gandhi smiled weakly.

Worried Indian politicians had hastily convened a Hindu Leaders' conference in Bombay to try to find a solution to the problem that would be acceptable to Gandhi. A major obstacle was the task of persuading Dr Ambedkar, who was especially keen on having separate electorates for the Untouchables. His people had suffered too long at the hands of caste Hindus, he felt, and needed to be protected. Ambedkar was reluctant to make any concessions.

Nevertheless, Ambedkar, together with other Hindu leaders, conferred directly with Gandhi at his bedside. Eventually, on the fifth day, a compromise was worked out, under which the Untouchables would have a number of reserved seats in parliament. It was a solution that Gandhi had previously been opposed to and Ambedkar expected him to oppose it now.

Everyone waited anxiously while the proposal was explained to Gandhi. He listened weakly — and agreed.

"But the British government must accept it too," he said, "before I end my fast."

The proposal was cabled to London. It was Sunday — and the Prime Minister had left London to go to the country for the day. All India waited and prayed. At last confirmation came that the proposal had been accepted.

Gandhi broke his fast on September 26 with a glass of orange juice.

The amendment to the new constitution was not the only outcome of Gandhi's fast. All over India, temples which for centuries had been reserved for caste Hindus were opened to Untouchables. Untouchables were allowed to get their water from public wells; Hindus and Untouchables ate together.

Although the problem of untouchability was not removed, Gandhi's fast resulted in the first breaking down of century old barriers.

16

A Place of Service

After his 'Epic Fast', Gandhi began to devote all his energy to improving the condition of the Untouchables — or the Harijans, as he now called them, 'The Children of God'.

An all-India organisation, Harijan Sevak Sangh, was established specially to help them. He also collaborated in setting up a new weekly journal called *Harijan* (his previous journal, *Young India*, had been suspended by the British), to which he regularly contributed articles on the problems of the Untouchables.

In this way, and by letters to the press, Gandhi worked hard to educate public opinion and to sustain the movement to eradicate some of the more unpleasant features of untouchability.

When he was released from prison in May 1933, Gandhi did not return to his home in the Sabarmati ashram. He gave this to the Harijan community. He himself went to live alone in Wardha, near Nagpur in Central India. But he was only there for a short time. In November he set off on a twelve thousand mile tour of India that lasted over nine months.

His target during this tour was both caste Hindus and Harijans. The former he urged to shake off their prejudices. It was nonsense, he argued, to believe that a person could be born 'unclean' or that someone could be 'defiled' by shadow or touch. The Harijans he tried to persuade to give up drink and drugs, with which many of them used to console themselves.

As he travelled through the provinces of India,

preaching and praying, Gandhi also collected money for a Harijan fund. The amount he managed to get in this way was not enormous, but in his view this did not matter: what was important was that thousands of people, rich and poor alike, from all castes, had contributed to it. It was a gesture of solidarity.

In October 1934 Gandhi formally resigned from the Congress Party, which he felt had grown a little tired of him. But his main purpose was to be free to devote all his energies to a programme of activities which would revitalise the villages, where 85% of India's population lived in near subsistence conditions.

Ever since he had returned from South Africa, Gandhi had become more and more convinced that the solution to India's economic problems lay in the villages.

'When I succeed in ridding the villages of poverty,' he wrote, 'I have won Swaraj!'

Ten years previously, he had founded the All India Spinners Association, which now reached into five thousand villages. This was an important achievement but, in spite of his obsession with spinning, which he forced on all those who came into contact with him, Gandhi realised that it did not provide all the answers. His nine month tour of India had brought home to him even more strongly how desperate the conditions in villages were.

He now launched a fresh campaign to get towns-people to buy not just goods 'Made in India' (in preference to ones made abroad), but ones that had been 'Made in Villages'. Every household used dozens of things, he argued, that could be made or processed in villages and it was the duty of people who lived in towns to buy these things — even if they cost a little more.

To support village products, the All India Village Industries Association was set up at the same Congress meeting as Gandhi sent his resignation.

As a gesture that was both practical and symbolic. Gandhi himself went to live in a village not far from Wardha, which was inhabited by a few hundred Untouchables. The name of the village at the time was Segaon. Gandhi chose it because it was poor and dirty. It had no proper roads or shops. The countryside around was bare, with very few trees.

Here Gandhi settled, alone, in a one room hut.

"If I can change Segaon," he argued, "then perhaps I can change the face of India."

It was not Gandhi's intention to set up another ashram like the one at Sabarmati, or to surround himself with followers. In fact he had intended to draw on the resources of the villagers themselves. But it was not long before he was joined in Segaon by disciples not only from India, but also from different parts of the world. These, all eager to help him, established a loose settlement around Gandhi's hut.

Segaon became a model for village welfare. A hospital was opened for the sick and a farm was started to make sure that there was a good supply of milk. A school was opened because Gandhi wanted to teach the young — to give them 'an all-round education, a good knowledge of Hindi or Urdu and, through that medium, of arithmetic and the rudiments of history and geography, a knowledge of simple scientific principles and some industrial training.'

Segaon became a laboratory for many of Gandhi's pet ideas: nutrition, agriculture, sanitation and education.

Gandhi's own way of life did not change in spite of the settlement that grew up around him. He divided his one big room into three smaller ones, but he had hardly any furniture. His 'desk' was an old soap box (the lettering could still be seen on it). Gandhi kept his complete 'library' in the bottom part. He owned only five books: the Bible, the Koran, the Gita, and his two favourite books by Ruskin and Tolstoi. People used to send him books from all over the world, but he gave them all away.

Next to his desk, Gandhi kept his beloved *charka* — his spinning wheel — which he never failed to use for half an hour every day. Sometimes important visitors came to see him. Gandhi received them with great courtesy, but he did not stop spinning until he had produced his quota of yarn.

The settlement itself was beautifully clean. It was Gandhi's idea that it should provide an example to the people of Segaon, who used to throw their rubbish straight into the street. He used to walk to the village every morning and sweep the streets himself. This was another way of setting the villagers an example.

He taught them how to plant vegetable gardens and how to spin and make cloth. It was an uphill task, he found.

"They refuse to learn anything!" he once exclaimed in despair. "They lack co-operation. They do not know the art of intelligent labour."

But slowly Segaon began to change.

There were at that time two villages with the same name. And because there was no post office in the Segaon where Gandhi lived, his mail sometimes went to the wrong place. So, in the end, the authorities decided to give Gandhi's village its own post office — and a new name.

"What would you like to call it?" Gandhi was asked. "Think of a name!"

Gandhi gave the matter a good deal of thought. Finally, he chose 'Sevagram' as the new name for his village. 'Sevagram' means 'place of service'.

Gandhi chose this name because here, in a small village in the centre of India, he and his helpers were trying to serve the whole of India.

17

Quit India!

On September 3 1939 Britain declared war on Germany. The same day the Viceroy, Lord Linlithgow, announced that India was at war too. At a stroke, as Nehru later observed, four hundred million people were plunged into war without any consultation at all.

Congress leaders were furious. Technically the Viceroy was within his rights to do this because matters of defence were the concern of the British government, but they felt that at least they should have been consulted.

Since the new constitution was introduced in 1937, Congress had co-operated with the British, even though the terms of the constitution were disappointing and unpopular. They had fought and won elections in six provinces. They had formed Congress governments, and on the whole, British and Indian administrators had learnt to get along with one another.

But, in spite of this high-handed treatment, most of the Congress leaders still supported Britain. A few days after the outbreak of war, the Working Committee condemned German aggression and announced that a 'free and democratic' India would join in the war. In short, India wanted independence in return for support.

Gandhi, who did not entirely agree with the line that Congress had taken, was summoned to Delhi to talk to the Viceroy. Lord Linlithgow felt unable to give any firm promises, but he hinted that there might be a change of status for India after the war. This was not enough for Congress. Four days later, provincial ministries were instructed to resign.

During the next year, while Hitler overran much of Europe, the search for common ground continued. Most Congress leaders would still have liked to support the war effort. But they demanded that Britain must declare unequivocally that India would gain her independence after the war in return for co-operation.

Again the Viceroy refused to make any firm promises. The status of India after the war, he argued, would have to be determined in consultation with other groups, such as Muslims, not with Congress alone. This was unacceptable to the Congress leaders.

In offering to support Britain conditionally, in return for independence, Congress had gone against Gandhi's wishes. Although he was now a convinced pacifist (and had discarded earlier ideas such as: 'A nation that is unfit to fight cannot from experience prove the virtue of not fighting'), he would have preferred to give Britain unconditional support.

But it was to Gandhi that Congress now looked for guidance. His advice was that they should mount a campaign of civil disobedience on grounds that had nothing to do with independence: namely, that even in wartime, Indians must be allowed the right of free speech in their own country.

This campaign, however, was to be different from earlier ones. The protest against restrictions on free speech was to be carried out by individuals. One by one, Congressmen were to stand up and make speeches against the war. One by one they would be arrested.

Nehru himself was one of the first to challenge the regulations. He was arrested and sent to prison for four years. By the end of the year, over four hundred Congressmen had been arrested for similar offences. In all, 25,000 members of the Congress party were sent to gaol.

The British viewed this civil disobedience campaign mainly as an irritation. As Gandhi himself had said, it was intended to be a symbolic act of protest rather than

85

a serious attempt to hinder the British war effort. In the end, all Congress prisoners were released.

Meanwhile, Japan entered the war. This was followed by the capture of Singapore and the invasion of first Malaysia and then Burma. Suddenly the war was on India's doorstep and Indian leaders began to be concerned for the safety of their country.

The British Prime Minister at the time was Winston Churchill, who disliked Gandhi and strongly opposed giving India her independence.

"I have not become the King's First Minister in order to preside at the liquidation of the British Empire, "he is reported to have said.

Yet even Churchill realised that it was necessary to attempt some reconciliation with the Indian leaders. After lengthy discussions in London with politicians who were familiar with the Indian political scene, Sir Stafford Cripps was sent out to Delhi with a draft plan.

Cripps was thought to be especially acceptable to the Indian leaders: he was a socialist, a vegetarian and he had visited India on his own account when war broke out. He had gone to see Gandhi in the ashram at Sevagram.

Cripps arrived in India on March 27 1942. He was highly optimistic about the success of his mission. Gandhi, however, who had been invited to Delhi to study the proposals, was not. 'A postdated cheque on a failing bank' was his comment. In fact, he suggested to Cripps that he should take the next plane home. Gandhi went back to Sevagram. Cripps stayed on in Delhi.

Gandhi's reaction foreshadowed that of other Indian leaders. The plan did provide for dominion status for India, like that of Canada and Australia, after the war. But India's constitution was to be worked out by an assembly, one third of whose members were to come from the princely states, where British influence, through the political advisers, was strong. Besides that,

86

any province of India would have the right not to become a member of the Indian Union and, in that case, the province would be granted autonomy. It hardly seemed likely that a united India would emerge from such a scheme!

Although all this was unacceptable to the Congress leaders, they would still have liked to work out a formula which would have given Indians themselves some responsibility for contributing to the war effort. But no agreement was reached and the talks broke down. Cripps flew back to London on April 12.

Gandhi's response to the failure of the Cripps mission was that India should demand independence immediately. This was the mood of the country and Gandhi probably sensed it. But, although he wanted power to be handed over to an Indian National Government, he did not envisage the British evacuating India completely. He accepted that British and Allied forces would need to remain in India and that the Indian National Government would have to collaborate with the British for the defence of the country.

In this respect Gandhi, as pragmatic as ever, had abandoned his earlier stand of non-involvement in the war.

Under Gandhi's guidance, the Congress Working Committee produced at a meeting on July 14 1942 their famous 'Quit India' resolution. 'British rule in India must cease immediately,' they declared. And if the British refused to respond to their demand, they proposed to launch a mass civil disobedience campaign.

The British had no intention of 'quitting' India at this point. Even if they had wished to, they were in no position to respond to the Indian request, with the Japanese at the very frontiers of India. Nor were they prepared to tolerate a mass civil disobedience campaign that would have disrupted the war effort.

The Viceroy moved quickly. On August 9 Gandhi,

Nehru and other key Indian politicians were arrested. Gandhi himself was imprisoned in the Aga Khan's Palace in Poona — in spite of his objection that he did not need such 'commodious' accommodation.

In reaction to Gandhi's arrest, a wave of violence swept the country. Rioting broke out in several provinces. Public buildings were burnt down. Officials were attacked. Railway lines and telegraph wires were sabotaged. The British responded brutally, often shooting into crowds.

Gandhi was appalled by the violence, but even more by official statements that he was responsible for it. He wrote to the Viceroy, protesting against the slaughter of people and the slaughter of truth. He asked to be allowed to see the Viceroy. The Viceroy declined, and continued to hold Gandhi responsible for the violence. Gandhi in his turn blamed the British government. Growl and counter-growl continued.

At this point Gandhi decided to go on a twenty-one day fast. The fast began on February 23 1943. Gandhi was seventy-three and no longer in good health. His condition deteriorated rapidily and after a few days the doctors who were attending him announced that they did not expect him to live.

The Viceroy was put under pressure to release Gandhi. He refused: he did not intend to submit to 'political blackmail', as he called it. Both he and the British government seemed ready to let Gandhi die.

Gandhi survived this twenty-one day fast, although his recovery afterwards was slow.

All the while, however, he kept up a constant flow of letters to the Viceroy and to the British government in London, disclaiming responsibility for the violence and sabotage that was sweeping the country. This was not the civil disobedience campaign he had planned. He had been arrested before he could launch one and in any case it would have been peaceful.

The Viceroy on his side continued to maintain the official view that Gandhi was to blame.

On previous occasions Gandhi had always been happy in prison. This time he was not. He suffered because India was suffering. He suffered because he could not protect himself from false propaganda. He also suffered because he lost two people who were close to him.

First, Mahadev Desai, who had been his secretary since 1917, died soon after Gandhi was imprisoned. Mahadev had been more than a meticulous secretary; he had been Gandhi's devoted companion and in many ways was more like a son to him.

Then, towards the end of 1943, Kasturbai fell ill. Her illness dragged on. Numerous doctors attended her, but she grew steadily worse. Penicillin might have saved her, but Gandhi refused the use of all drugs not only for himself but also on those around him.

Kasturbai died, with her head in her husband's lap. on February 22 1944.

"I cannot imagine life without Ba," Gandhi said. "We lived together for sixty-two years. We were a couple outside the ordinary."

Their married life had not always been peaceful. But Gandhi had come to depend on her more and more, even if sometimes she seemed to be only a shadowy figure at his shoulder, rarely speaking or spoken to. She looked after the domestic side of the ashram — even Gandhi himself did not dare to interfere in that — and she involved herself in his political campaigns. She had even learnt how to go to gaol. But, to the end, she remained stubbornly independent, even breaking ashram rules when she chose.

One cause of domestic discontent was Gandhi's harsh and inflexible attitude towards his own children. He never indulged them, like other fathers, nor did he find time to play with them, as he did later in life with other people's children. He had persistently denied them any regular education — despite their protests that he was cutting them off from the professional advantages he had got for himself.

Harilal, the eldest, rebelled against his father completely. When the family went back to South Africa for the second time, he stayed on in India to study. Later, he married against his father's wishes and was disowned. After his wife's death Harilal took to drink and became involved in a series of business ventures, many of a somewhat dubious kind, that were a constant source of embarrassment to his parents. Gandhi protested publicly that he still loved his son but wrote, in an article in Young India: 'Men may be good, not necessarily their children.'

Even Manilal, Gandhi's second son, who was much closer to his father, incurred his displeasure. On one occasion, he used ashram funds to help Harilal in one of his business enterprises. When Gandhi found out, he 'banished' Manilal to South Africa. Manilal returned to India only once during his father's lifetime.

Shortly after Kasturbai's death, Gandhi himself became seriously ill. The doctors diagnosed a number of diseases and, although he gradually recovered, his general physical condition remained weak, and the British decided that it would be safer to release him from gaol.

Gandhi never went to prison again. Altogether he had spent more than six years of his life in gaol: two hundred and forty nine days in South Africa and two thousand and eighty-nine in India.

18

Independence

The year: 1945. The war in Europe and Asia was over and, in England, the newly elected Labour government, led by Clement Attlee (who as a junior politician had been a member of the commission that had visited India in 1927), was resolved to give India its independence.

Early in 1946 a parliamentary delegation was sent out to India. Independence — for which Indians had been struggling for nearly half a century — was at last in sight.

But there were many obstacles. The Muslim league, led by Mohamed Ali Jinnah, was insisting more firmly than ever on a separate state for Muslims. Gandhi, on the other hand, wanted to keep India united and on the whole the British delegation favoured this too. But, at the same time, it wanted to find a solution that was quick and also met with everyone's approval.

There was a good deal of unrest in the country at the time. Indian troops had already come close to mutiny. The war had brought quick wealth to a few, but for most it meant higher prices and food shortages. Bengal had already suffered a famine, in the course of which, according to official estimates, a million and a half people had died.

The situation was already tense when the Muslim League called for a 'Direct Action' day on August 16 1946. In the communal riots that followed, Muslims butchered Hindus and Hindus butchered Muslims. On a single day of violence in Calcutta more than five thousand people died.

91

Gandhi was in Delhi when he heard the news of the violence in Bengal. He decided to go at once to Calcutta, which was the centre of some of the worst trouble, to see for himself.

"I am unable to discover the truth," he said, after he had tried to inquire into the reasons for the killings. "But there is terrible mistrust."

To try to restore some peace to the two communities, Gandhi went to live in a small village in East Bengal. It was a largely Muslim village; the Hindus who had once lived there had fled when trouble broke out. Gandhi spent six weeks in the village, living his usual life of prayer and hard work, but at the same time talking hard to members of the Muslim community. Gradually peace returned.

In January 1947 Gandhi announced that he would begin a tour of East Bengal on foot.

"I will walk through Bengal," he said, "and I will speak to every Indian I meet. And I will teach him about peace and love."

After a lifetime of preaching non-violence, this was the only way Gandhi could see of getting his message across.

So, at the age of seventy-seven, barefooted, he set off on a pilgrimage through Bengal. Villages were burning and everywhere people were fighting and killing one another. Unafraid, Gandhi continued to preach his message of peace.

Two months later, he did the same in the province of Bihar, where Hindus had savagely attacked Muslim minorities.

Meanwhile, a thousand miles away in Delhi, while Gandhi was trying to bring peace back to Bengal and Bihar, Indian politicians continued to wrangle.

Finally, in February 1947, the British government announced a date for Indian independence: 'not later than June 1948'. At the same time, a new Viceroy, Lord Louis Mountbatten, was appointed to make the final arrangements for the transfer of power.

Mountbatten had intensive talks with all the Indian leaders, including Gandhi, who was called back from Bihar for consultations. The partition of India, and the creation of a new state for Muslims, to be called Pakistan, was now regarded as inevitable. Gandhi was still opposed in principle to partition, but he did not oppose the final plan.

Recognising that he could not do anything further to stop India from being divided, he now concentrated his whole attention on practical problems. The division of India into two countries meant that millions of people would have to leave their homes. Families and lives would be disrupted. Gandhi's final judgement on partition was in terms of human suffering rather than political values.

Gandhi did not stay in Delhi to join in the celebrations for Independence Day on August 15 1947. He had already left for East Bengal, where further violence was anticipated. He got as far as Calcutta, where he decided to stay in the house of a poor Muslim workman in a neighbourhood that was almost entirely Hindu.

Soon he was surrounded by angry Hindu demonstrators, unable to understand his support for their Muslim enemies. But Gandhi not only managed to pacify the mob. He also persuaded Hindus and Muslims to celebrate Independence Day together.

But peace between the two communities was fragile. Violence broke out again when news of massacres of Hindus in the Punjab reached Calcutta. At one point, Gandhi's own life was in danger. His answer to the violence was to announce a fast that would continue until all violence stopped.

This had the desired effect, and Calcutta was soon calm again. Later, even when there was trouble in the rest of India, Hindus and Muslims respected the promises they had given to Gandhi.

In the Punjab, however, which was the other big

93

province split in two by partition, violence increased as refugees poured from one part to the other. Frequently fights broke out between groups going in opposite directions to their new homes. Gandhi decided that this was where his help was now needed.

But he got no further than Delhi, which was full of refugees from the newly created state of Pakistan and torn apart by rioting. Many of the Hindu refugees wanted to seize the houses and shops of Muslims who stayed on in India, as recompense for the ones they had themselves lost.

In the following months, Gandhi worked hard to bring peace back to the city. He organised voluntary aid for the refugees and slowly an uneasy calm returned to the city. But still he was not satisfied. He felt that he had managed to contain the fire, but it might at any moment burst out again. Muslims were only safe so long as they remained shut up in their houses.

In January 1948, Gandhi announced that he would begin another fast — a fast that would continue until all the Muslims in Delhi were safe; until they felt that they could walk through the streets as freely as himself.

Many Hindus were furious with him. They could not understand why he wanted to help the Muslims in this way.

"Hindus aren't safe in Pakistan," they pointed out. "Why don't you go to Pakistan and fast there?"

Gandhi agreed: he was ready to go to Pakistan. But first he had to protect the Muslims in India.

Gandhi began his fast on January 13. His doctors gave him six days to live. By the third day he was already weak.

Gandhi chose that moment to ask the Indian government to pay to Pakistan a large sum of money that was being withheld. The money was promptly paid.

Meanwhile, leaders of all the communal groups had been meeting to try to find a way to persuade Gandhi to end his fast. It was agreed that some kind of pledge was needed which, when taken, would bind their followers to protect Muslims. The form of the pledge was explained to Gandhi on the morning of January 18.

Gandhi was barely satisfied but, with some misgivings, because he felt that the pledge should cover Muslims all over India, he broke his fast with a glass of orange juice.

The lives of the Muslims were now safe for a time, but Gandhi had put his own life in danger. Certain fanatical Hindus hated him for the support he gave to Muslims. Within two days, an attempt was made on his life when a home-made bomb went off at one of his prayer meetings.

The police suspected a conspiracy and wanted to protect him. Gandhi refused.

"You are wrong in believing that you can protect me," he said. "God is my protector."

Perhaps he already knew that his death was near, although he often joked that he wanted to live until he was a hundred and twenty-five years old.

His self-appointed assassin was Nathuram Vinayak Godse, a thirty-seven year old Brahmin from Poona and a member of a right wing Hindu group. Godse decided 'to take the extreme step against Gandhi' because he believed he had betrayed Hindus to the Muslims.

Godse, with his accomplices, hung around Birla House for several days. On January 30, armed with a small pistol, he mingled with the crowd that had come to Gandhi's prayer meeting and had no difficulty in getting within point blank range of the mahatma.

Soon all India heard the terrible news when Prime Minister Nehru broadcast to the nation.

"The light has gone out of our lives and there is darkness everywhere and I do not quite know what to tell you and how to say it. Our beloved leader, Bapu as we call him, the father of our nation, is no more."

19

No Ordinary Light

"The light has gone out," Prime Minister Nehru continued in his broadcast to the Indian nation shortly after Gandhi's death, "and yet I was wrong. For the light that shone in this country was no ordinary light. The light that has illumined this country for these many years will illumine this country for many more years, and a thousand years later that light will still be seen in this country, and the world will see it and it will give solace to innumerable hearts. For that light represented the living truth, and the eternal man was with us with his eternal truth, reminding us of the right path, drawing us from error, taking this ancient country to freedom."

The question has often been asked: was Gandhi a saint — or a politician? Gandhi himself was well aware of the debate, which started early on in his career.

"Men say I am a saint losing myself in politics," he responded. "The fact is I am a politician trying my hardest to be a saint."

All his life Gandhi worked hard to perfect his spiritual qualities.

"What I want to achieve," he wrote in the introduction to his autobiography, *The Story of My Experiments with Truth*, "what I have been striving to achieve these thirty years, is self realization, to see God face to face . . . All that I do by way of speaking and writing, and all my ventures in the political field, are directed to this same end."

Hence Gandhi's decision to practise *brahmacharya*,

to lead a life of total abstinence from the age of thirty-six. He wanted to be free to devote all his energies to his chosen way of life.

But, unlike many Indian holy men, Gandhi did not believe that he could attain *moksha*, or salvation, by cutting himself off from his fellow men and retreating to a cave in the Himalayas. He believed that he could attain salvation through a life of action, through helping people.

Gandhi could never shake off the title of *mahatma* — great soul — which Tagore had given him early on, but he never quite accepted it either. The masses, especially those who lived in the villages, would have liked to worship him as a holy man. But Gandhi rejected this kind of 'deification'. If people believed that he had spiritual powers, they would expect him to change their lives by working miracles. Gandhi wanted them to change their lives through their own efforts. The settlement of Sevagram was intended to provide a living example of what could be achieved through hard work.

As a politician, Gandhi's chief goal was social reform. In South Africa, he had fought for the rights of Indians on the grounds that they were members of the British Empire. Back in India, in spite of his deep admiration for the empire as an institution — he believed at the time that it actually benefited India — he quickly realised that the British were opposed to any real social reform. It was not in their interests to change a system which worked to their advantage. The British had to leave India, therefore. Thus, the struggle for social reform became the struggle for independence.

Gandhi organised the struggle for independence around one central idea: *satyagraha*. He had already tested and established the effectiveness of *satyagraha* as a political weapon in South Africa and, as soon as he had settled down in India, he began to train his *satyagrahis* there too. His ashram at Sabarmati was both a place of retreat and a training camp.

The series of experiments that followed were not always successful: sometimes violence broke out. His fellow politicians too were often impatient with him: some wanted tougher action and quicker results. It took nearly fifteen years for Gandhi to demonstrate the effectiveness of *satyagraha* through the breaking of the salt laws. Its ultimate success, however, in gaining India her independence, brought little satisfaction: the communal riots showed that the lesson of non-violence had not really been learnt.

Although Gandhi saw himself as a politician, his involvement in politics was almost accidental. Had he stayed in India as a young man, he might have remained a competent but obscure writer of legal briefs. Even in South Africa, where like many of his fellow Indians he went to make some money —'to try my luck', as he said — he might have ended up as a successful barrister.

Instead, his experience on the train at Maritzburg completely changed the course of his life. Suddenly, as a result of his stand against injustice, Gandhi found leadership thrust upon him. His great sense of moral purpose appealed to the Indian community, so that in the end they too were carried away by his ideas. Few Indian traders could have anticipated that they would one day be suffering all the hardships and deprivation of a *satyagraha* campaign.

And then his willingness to work for the underprivileged, the imported labourers, gave him a platform of popular support. By the time he returned to India, he had already made a name for himself, and he was able to enter politics alongside experienced Congressmen — and in a few years to emerge as their acknowledged leader.

In spite of his unorthodox methods, Gandhi was a skilful politician, as Nehru acknowledged when he called him a 'magician'. He demonstrated his ability to move people again and again — when he fasted;

when he faced angry rioting crowds in Calcutta and when he walked through Bengal and Bihar.

But his real secret, perhaps, was not so much magic as a concern for people. Gandhi interpreted his political mission in human terms. Hence his preoccupation with India's poor, the millions who lived in the villages — which his fellow politicians at the time were scarcely aware of — and with the Muslims at the time of partition.

But not everyone admired the 'Gandhian' approach to politics. The British were puzzled by him because he appeared to be inconsistent — especially when he was listening for guidance to his 'inner voice'. He irritated many of his fellow politicians because he did not value material progress. His attitude towards machines and industrialisation made many Indians uneasy. Was Gandhi trying to put the clock back, they wondered, with his preoccupation with villages and his campaign for buying village products and wearing *khadi*? To many it seemed that Gandhi was simply ignoring the harsh economic realities of modern life.

Yet, in spite of his own deep convictions, Gandhi was never dogmatic: people were free to accept or reject his most treasured ideas.

"Never take anything for gospel truth," he once said, "even if it comes from a *mahatma!*"

Gandhi's life was a series of experiments in search of truth, both in his public and private life. He did not claim to be an intellectual, or to have original ideas.

"I have nothing new to tell the world," he once wrote. "Truth and non-violence are as old as the hills."

To people who looked to him for a 'message', he had a very simple answer.

"Study my life," he told them. "My life is my message."

20

A Calendar of main events
in the life of Gandhi

1869   Born in Porbandar (Western India) on October 2.

1882   Married to Kasturbai at the age of thirteen.

1888   Goes to England to study law.

1891   Returns to India, (aged 21) qualified as a barrister.

1893   Goes to work in South Africa and experiences racial prejudice at Maritzburg. Organises Indians in Pretoria to resist racial discrimination.

1894   Invited to stay in Natal to fight anti-Indian legislation. Organises opposition and becomes known as protector of the poor Indian labourers.

1896   Returns to India to fetch his family. Makes speeches about South Africa problem. Is attacked by white mob on his return to South Africa. Continues the fight for the rights of Indians for the next three years, but also establishes himself as a successful lawyer.

1900   Organises ambulance relief work on behalf of the British in their fight against the Boers (1899–1902).

1901   Returns to India and sets up law practice in Bombay. Makes contact with Indian political leaders.

1902 Called back to South Africa and resumes fight against repression.

1904 Sets up Phoenix Farm, his first experiment in community living.

1906 Organises resistance to the Registration Act and teaches non-violent resistance. The struggle continues over the next few years.

1911 Establishes Tolstoi Farm as a refuge for his *satyagrahis* (non-violent resistance fighters).

1912 Gokhale, a leading Indian politician, visits South Africa. Smuts promises to repeal the Registration Act (but does not).

1913 Cape Colony Supreme Court declares non-Christian marriages illegal. Gandhi, helped by Indian women, organises resistance. World opinion obliges South Africa to negotiate rights for Indian community.

1914 Gandhi visits England at outbreak of First World War (1914–1918), in which India helps Britain with money and troops.

1915 Returns to India (at the age of forty-five) and tours the country to get to know India's problems. Sets up the Sabarmati ashram near Ahmedabad.

1917 Intervenes in dispute between peasants and landlords in Bihar and in dispute between workers and millowners in Ahmedabad. First political fast and the beginning of *satyagraha* in India.

1918 Organises peasant resistance to the British government in Kheda.

1919 Rowlatt Act restricts Indian civil liberties. Gandhi organises all India one day peaceful strike. Jallianwalla massacre in Amritsar.

1920 Gandhi initiates non co-operation campaign.

1921   Tours India to explain non co-operation pro-
       gramme.

1922   Policemen murdered at Chauri Chaura. Gandhi
       arrested for sedition and, at the 'Great Trial' in
       Ahmedabad, sentenced to six years in prison.

1924   Released from gaol. Fast on behalf of Hindu-
       Muslim unity.

1924   Gandhi 'retires' from politics and, for three
       years, devotes himself to campaign of social
       improvement in the rural areas.

1928   British parliamentary commission visits India to
       review constitutional position. Boycotted by
       Congress politicians, who demand dominion
       status within twelve months.

1929   Congress passes resolution in favour of inde-
       pendence.

1930   Gandhi calls on Indians to break the Salt Law
       and leads Salt March to Dandi. Mass arrests in
       India. Gandhi sent back to prison.

1931   Gandhi (aged 62) goes to London to attend
       Round Table Conference. Great success with
       British public.

1932   Returns to India to find renewal of British
       repression. Sent back to prison. 'Epic Fast'
       against separate electorate for Untouchables.

1933   Released from prison. Tours India to speak on
       behalf of the Untouchables.

1934   Resigns from Congress. Settles at Segaon (later
       Sevagram) near Nagpur in Central India, from
       where he continues programme of social
       reform.

1939   Outbreak of Second World War (1939–1945).
       Viceroy announces that India is also at war.

1940   Indian political leaders wage civil disobedience
       campaign against loss of civil liberties.

1942   Failure of Cripps mission to discuss post-war
        status for India. Congress passes 'Quit India'
        resolution. Outbreak of violence after arrest of
        Gandhi and other leading politicians.

1943   Gandhi fasts for 21 days against accusation of
        responsibility for violence.

1944   Death of Kasturbai. Gandhi (now aged 74)
        released from prison.

1945   Labour government in Britain announces that
        India will be given independence.

1946   Parliamentary mission sent to India to work out
        new constitution. Muslim leader, Jinnah,
        demands separate state for Muslims. 'Direct
        Action' day followed by riots and killings in
        Bengal and Bihar. Gandhi walks through
        Bengal and Bihar to try to restore peace.

1947   India becomes independent on August 15.

1948   Gandhi undertakes final fast to win safety for
        Muslims in India. Assassinated on January 30
        while going to attend a prayer meeting in the
        gardens of Birla House.

Select Bibliography

This short list of books is intended as a guide for the general reader who is interested in finding out more about Gandhi. It includes only titles that are likely to be widely available.

M.K. Gandhi *An Autobiography or The Story of my Experiments with Truth* (Penguin (for Navajivan Press) 1982)

Ronald Duncan *Selected Writings of Mahatma Gandhi* (Fontana 1971)

Louis Fischer *The Life of Mahatma Gandhi* (Granada 1982)

B.R. Nanda *Mahatma Gandhi. A biography* (Oxford University Press (India) 1981)

Chandra Kumar & Mohinder Puri *Mahatma Gandhi. His Life and Influence* (Heinemann 1982)

Ved Mehta *Mahatma Gandhi and His Apostles* (Penguin 1977)

R.K. Narayan *Waiting for the Mahatma* (A novel) (Methuen 1955)